Just Look 'n Learn
GERMAN
PICTURE DICTIONARY

1,500 Words for Beginning German Learners

Learn to Tell Time– Learn to Count

Illustrations and Example Sentences for Each Entry

Illustrated by
Daniel J. Hochstatter

McGraw-Hill

*New York   Chicago   San Francisco   Lisbon   London   Madrid   Mexico City
Milan   New Delhi   San Juan   Seoul   Singapore   Sydney   Toronto*

Who is in this book?

Thomas
Thomas

Tante Alice
Aunt Alice

Onkel Eduard
Uncle Edward

Maria
Mary

Susanne
Susan

Mutter und Vater
Mother and Father

Großvater und Großmutter
Grandfather and Grandmother

Robert
Robert

Helene
Helen

Jimmy
Jimmy

Wilhelm
William

Stephan
Steven

Library of Congress Cataloging-in-Publication Data

Just Look 'n Learn German picture dictionary / illustrated by Daniel J. Hochstatter.
     p.   cm.
    Includes index.
    ISBN 0-07-140831-2
    1. Picture dictionaries, German.   I. Hochstatter, Daniel J.
  PF3629.J87   1996
  433'.21—dc20
                         96-9659
                         CIP

What is in this book?

The *Words and Pictures* start on the next page.

Each entry shows how someone who lives in a place where German is spoken would say the English word and example sentence in German.

blue
blau

Der
Schmetterling ist blau.
The butterfly is blue.

There are many *Numbers* to learn on pages 82 and 83.

Learn the *Days of the Week* on page 84.

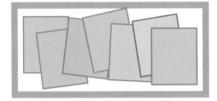

See the names of the *Months* on page 85.

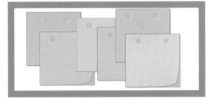

The names of different *Shapes* are on page 86.

Learn about *Compass Directions* on page 87.

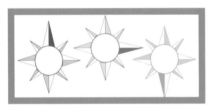

Try telling *Time* on page 88.

When you see an ✳ in the dictionary, look for the *Irregular English Words* on page 88.

be*

An *Index* to the German Words starts on page 89.

AaAaAaAa

above
über

Eine Lampe
hängt über
dem Tisch.
A lamp hangs
above the table.

acorn
die Eichel

Die Eichhörnchen
essen Eicheln gern.
The squirrels love to eat acorns.

acrobat
der Akrobat
die Akrobatin

Die Akrobatin
geht auf
ihren Händen.
The acrobat
walks on her hands.

actions
die Handlungen

Thomas
lachte
über die
Handlungen
des Clowns.
Thomas laughed
at the clown's actions.

---

actor
der Schauspieler

Der
Schauspieler
ist im
Rampenlicht.
The actor is in the spotlight.

actress
die Schauspielerin

Die Schauspielerin
ist am Fernsehen.
The actress is on television.

add
zufügen

Füge die Milch
dem Müsli zu.
Add the milk to the cereal.

address
die Adresse

Die Adresse
ist auf dem
Paket.
The address is
on the package.

after
nach

Wir spielen Ball
nach der Schule.
We play ball after school.

air
die Luft

Kalte Luft
kommt durch
das Fenster.
Cold air is coming in the window.

---

airplane
das Flugzeug

Das Flugzeug
fliegt durch Wolken.
The airplane is flying through clouds.

alarm clock
der Wecker

Susannes
Wecker steht
auf dem Nachttisch.
Susan's alarm clock
is on the night table.

alike
gleich

Die Blumen
sehen gleich aus.
The flowers look alike.

all
alle

Alle Blätter sind gefallen.
All the leaves have fallen.

alligator
der Alligator

Der Alligator
kletterte aus dem Fluß.
The alligator climbed out of the river.

alphabet
das Alphabet

Die Studentin
schrieb das
Alphabet.
The student wrote the alphabet.

always
immer

Das Baby lächelt immer.
The baby always smiles.

ambulance
**der Kranken-
wagen**

Ein Kranken-
wagen
raste die
Straße hinab.

An ambulance
raced down the street.

anchor
der Anker

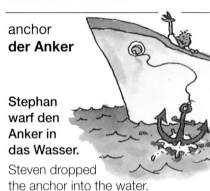

Stephan
warf den
Anker in
das Wasser.

Steven dropped
the anchor into the water.

angel
der Engel

Engel
haben Flügel.

Angels have wings.

angry
ärgerlich

Thomas macht
ein ärgerliches
Gesicht.

Thomas is making
an angry face.

animal
das Tier

Viele Tiere leben im Zoo.

Many animals live at the zoo.

ant
die Ameise

Die Ameisen
krochen in die
Zuckerschale.

The ants crawled
into the sugar bowl.

apple
der Apfel

In diesem
Apfel ist ein Wurm.

This apple has a worm in it.

apricot
die Aprikose

Aprikosen
wachsen
auf Bäumen.

Apricots grow on trees.

apron
die Schürze

An der
Schürze des
Koches ist Senf.

The cook's apron
has mustard on it.

aquarium
das Aquarium

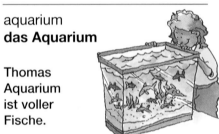

Thomas
Aquarium
ist voller
Fische.

Thomas's
aquarium is full of fish.

archer
der Bogenschütze

Ein Bogenschütze
trägt einen Bogen und Pfeile.

An archer carries a bow and arrows.

arm
der Arm

Ein Rotkehlchen
sitzt auf
Helenes Arm.

A robin is sitting
on Helen's arm.

armchair
der Sessel

Der neue
Sessel ist
bequem.

The new armchair is comfortable.

around
um

Ein Zaun geht um unser Haus.

A fence goes around our house.

arrow
der Pfeil

Der Pfeil
weist auf
die Tür.

The arrow
points to the door.

arrowhead
die Pfeilspitze

Ich fand
eine
Pfeilspitze
in dem Feld.

I found an arrowhead in the field.

art
die Kunst

Kunst wird
im Museum
aufbewahrt.

Art is kept at the museum.

artist
**der
Künstler
die
Künstlerin**

Der Künst-
ler malt ein
Bild von dem Ozean.

The artist is painting
a picture of the ocean.

astronaut
der Astronaut
die Astronautin

Der Astronaut
stand auf
dem Mond.

The astronaut
stood on the moon.

at
zu

Jimmy ist
den ganzen Tag zu Hause.

Jimmy is at home all day.

athlete
der Athlet
die Athletin

Der Athlet gewann
eine Goldmedaille.

The athlete won
a gold medal.

attic
die Dachstube

Großmutters
Haus hat
eine Dachstube.

Grandma's house has an attic.

aunt
die Tante

Thomas
Tante ist die
Schwester
seines Vaters.

Thomas's aunt is his father's sister.

autumn
der Herbst

Im Herbst harken wir Blätter.

In the autumn we rake leaves.

avocado
die Avokato

Maria aß eine
Avokato zum Mittagessen.

Mary ate an avocado for lunch.

away
weg

Der Hase
rannte weg.

The rabbit ran away.

ax
die Axt

Der Farmer
fällt den
Baum mit
einer Axt.

The farmer
is cutting the
tree down with an ax.

BbBbBbBb

baby
das Baby

Das Baby spielt mit Spielzeugen.
The baby is playing with toys.

back
die Rückseite
Susanne
hat einen
Reißverschluß
auf der Rückseite
ihres Kleides.

Susan has a zipper
on the back of her dress.

backpack
der Rucksack

Viele Studenten
tragen
Rucksäcke
zur Schule.

Many students wear
backpacks to school.

bad
schlecht

Das Wetter
war zu
schlecht für
ein Picknick.

The weather was
too bad for a picnic.

badminton
das Federball-spiel

Wir spielten
Federball auf dem Hof.
We played badminton in the yard.

bag
der Beutel

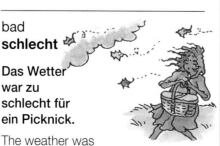

Wilhelm
steckt einen
Apfel in
seinen Lunchbeutel.

William puts an apple
into his lunch bag.

baggage
das Gepäck

Unser Gepäck
war schwer!
Our baggage
was heavy!

bake
backen

Meine Mama backte Brot für mich.

My mom baked some bread for me.

baker
der Bäcker

Der Bäcker ist glücklich.

The baker is happy.

bakery
die Bäckerei

Onkel Eduard kauft Brot in der Bäckerei.

Uncle Edward buys bread at the bakery.

ball
der Ball

Mein neuer Ball ist auf dem Dach.

My new ball is on the roof.

balloon
der Ballon

Der Ballon des Jungen ist zu seinem Handgelenk festgebunden.

The boy's balloon is tied to his wrist.

banana
die Banane

Ich esse Bananen zu meinem Müsli.

I have bananas with my cereal.

band
die Kapelle

Die Kapelle spielt im Park.

The band is playing in the park.

bandage
der Verband

Robert hat einen Verband an seinem Arm.

Robert has a bandage on his arm.

bang
der Knall

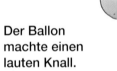

Der Ballon machte einen lauten Knall.

The balloon made a loud bang.

bangs
die Ponyhaare

Helenes Ponyhaare hängen ihr über der Stirn.

Helen's bangs hang down over her forehead.

bank
die Bank

Ich bringe mein Geld zur Bank.

I take my money to the bank.

banner
die Fahne

Ich trug eine rot-goldene Fahne in der Parade.

I carried a red and gold banner in the parade.

barbecue
der Grill

Er kochte Huhn auf dem Grill.

He cooked chicken on the barbecue.

barbecue
grillen

Onkel Eduard grillte ein Huhn zum Abendessen.

Uncle Edward barbecued a chicken for dinner.

barber
der Friseur

Die Scheren des Friseurs sind scharf.

The barber's scissors are sharp.

barn
die Scheune

Der Farmer hält seine Kühe in der Scheune.

The farmer keeps his cows in the barn.

barrel
das Faß

Ich könnte ein Faß Limonade trinken!

I could drink a barrel of lemonade!

barrette
die Spange

Maria trägt eine Spange in ihrem langen Haar.

Mary wears a barrette in her long hair.

baseball
der Baseball

Wilhelm fing den Baseball.
William caught the baseball.

basket
der Korb

Der Korb ist
voll mit Eiern.
The basket is full of eggs.

basketball
das Basket-ballspiel

Die Studenten spielen Basketball.
The students are playing basketball.

bat
die Fledermaus

Fledermäuse
wohnen in der Höhle.
Bats live in the cave.

bat
der Schläger

Robert traf den Baseball
mit seinem neuen Schläger.
Robert hit the baseball
with his new bat.

bath
das Bad

Jimmy
nimmt ein Bad.
Jimmy is taking a bath.

bathe
baden

Mutter
badet
das Baby
Jimmy oft.
Mother bathes baby Jimmy often.

bathing suit
der Badeanzug

Mein
Badeanzug
ist grün.
My bathing suit is green.

bathrobe
der Bademantel

Meine Mama
hat einen alten
purpurfarbenen
Bademantel.
My mom has an
old, purple bathrobe.

bathroom
das Badezimmer

Das Badezimmer
ist sauber.
The bathroom is clean.

bathtub
die Badewanne

Die Kinder spielten
in der Badewanne.
The children played in the bathtub.

bay
die Bucht

Die Boote in
der Bucht sind sicher.
The boats in the bay are safe.

be*
sein

Du wirst
bald groß sein.
You will be tall soon.

beach
der Strand

Weißer Sand
bedeckt den Strand.
White sand covers the beach.

beak
der Schnabel

Ein Vogel
frißt mit
seinem Schnabel.
A bird eats with its beak.

bear
der Bär

Ein brauner
Bär rannte aus
dem Wald.
A brown bear
ran out of the forest.

bear cub
das Bärenjunge

Die Bärenjungen
kletterten auf
den Baum.
The bear cubs
climbed a tree.

beard
der Bart

Stephans Großvater hat einen langen, grauen Bart.

Steven's grandfather has a long, gray beard.

beautiful
schön

Susannes Partykleid ist schön.

Susan's party dress is beautiful.

beaver
der Biber

Der Biber hat einen flachen Schwanz.

The beaver has a flat tail.

become*
werden

Susanne wird groß.

Susan is becoming tall.

bed
das Bett

Mein Bett ist zu weich.

My bed is too soft.

bedroom
das Schlafzimmer

Marias Schlafzimmer hat zwei Betten.

Mary's bedroom has two beds in it.

bee
die Biene

Bienen machen Honig.

Bees make honey.

behind
hinter

Der große Junge stand hinter seinem Bruder.

The tall boy stood behind his brother.

bell
die Klingel

Stephan läutet die Klingel zum Abendessen.

Steven rings the bell for dinner.

below
unter

Wasser fließt unter der Brücke.

Water runs below the bridge.

belt
der Gürtel

Stephans Gürtel ist zu weit für seine Hosen.

Steven's belt is too wide for his pants.

bench
die Bank

Der Hund schläft auf der Bank.

The dog is sleeping on the bench.

beneath
unter

Mein Bett ist unter dem meines Bruders.

My bed is beneath my brother's.

beside
neben

Der Hund saß neben meinem Stuhl.

The dog sat beside my chair.

best*
der Beste

Der beste Athlet gewinnt einen Preis.

The best athlete wins a prize.

better*
besser

Susanne ist eine bessere Läuferin als Wilhelm.

Susan is a better runner than William.

between
zwischen

Meine Tante sitzt zwischen mir und meiner Schwester.

My aunt sits between me and my sister.

bicycle
das Fahrrad

Susanne fährt oft mit dem Fahrrad zur Schule.

Susan often rides her bicycle to school.

big
groß

Das
ist ein
großer
Kuchen!
This is a big cake!

big top
das Zirkuszelt

Der Zirkus
spielt im Zirkuszelt.
The circus is under the big top.

bill
der Schnabel

Der
Vogelschnabel ist orange.
The bird's bill is orange.

bill
die (Bank) note

Thomas
fand eine
Fünf-Dollar-Note.
Thomas found a five-dollar bill.

binoculars
das Fernglas

Robert
sieht
durch
das Fernglas.
Robert is looking
through the binoculars.

bird
der Vogel

Der Vogel
saß auf
dem Baum.
The bird sat in the tree.

birthday
der Geburtstag

Mein Bruder hatte eine
Party an seinem Geburtstag.
My brother had a party
on his birthday.

birthday cake
der Geburtstagskuchen

Auf
meinem
Geburtstagskuchen sind Kerzen.
My birthday cake has candles on it.

bite* (nibble)
knabbern

Höre auf,
an deinen
Fingernägel
zu knabbern.
Stop biting your fingernails.

bite
der Bissen

Willst du mir
einen Bissen geben?
Will you give me a bite?

black
schwarz

Mein Vater
trägt einen
schwarzen
Anzug zur Arbeit.
My father wears a black suit to work.

blackboard
die Tafel

Helene
wird die
Tafel wischen.
Helen will clean the blackboard.

blanket
die Bettdecke

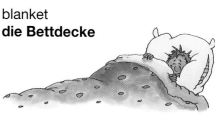

Meine Bettdecke hält mich warm.
My blanket keeps me warm.

block
der Häuserblock

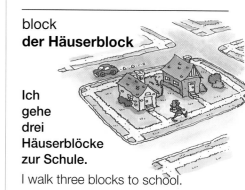

Ich
gehe
drei
Häuserblöcke
zur Schule.
I walk three blocks to school.

block
der Baustein

Meine kleine
Schwester spielt mit Bausteinen.
My little sister plays with blocks.

blossom
die Blüte

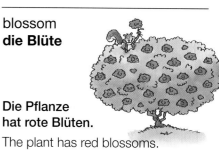

Die Pflanze
hat rote Blüten.
The plant has red blossoms.

blouse
die Bluse

Ich habe
eine Bluse,
die zu
meinem
Rock paßt.
I have a blouse
to go with my skirt.

blow*
blasen

Der Wind blies unseren Drachen am Himmel herum.

The wind blew our kite around the sky.

blue
blau

Der Schmetterling ist blau.

The butterfly is blue.

blush
erröten

Helene errötete, als ihr Name aufgerufen wurde.

Helen blushed when her name was called.

board
das Brett

Der Bauer sägte Bretter um den Zaun zu reparieren.

The farmer sawed boards to fix the fence.

boat
das Boot

Wilhelm segelte sein Boot auf dem Teich.

William sailed his boat on the pond.

body
der Körper

Man wäscht seinen Körper in der Badewanne.

You wash your body in the bathtub.

bone
der Knochen

Der Hund trug den Knochen zu seiner Hütte.

The dog carried the bone to his house.

book
das Buch

Stephan liest ein Buch.

Steven is reading a book.

bookcase
der Bücherschrank

Der Bücherschrank ist voll.

The bookcase is full.

boot
der Stiefel

Ich trage Stiefel wenn es schneit.

I wear boots when it snows.

both
beide

Beide Äpfel sind rot.

Both apples are red.

bottle
die Flasche

Medizin ist oft in einer Flasche.

Medicine often comes in a bottle.

bottom
unter

Wilhelm öffnete die untere Schublade.

William opened the bottom drawer.

boulder
der Felsblock

Eine Felsblock fiel in der Nähe des Autos.

A boulder fell near the car.

bouquet
der Strauß

Ich gab Großmutter einen großen Blumenstrauß.

I gave Grandma a big bouquet of flowers.

bow
sich verbeugen

Stephan verbeugt sich vor dem Publikum.

Steven is bowing to the audience.

bow
die Schleife

Eine große Schleife war auf dem Paket.

There was a large bow on the package.

bowl
die Schüssel

Thomas aß eine Schüssel voll Müsli.

Thomas ate a bowl of cereal.

box
die Schachtel

Das Geschenk kam in einer großen Schachtel.

The gift came in a big box.

boy
der Junge

Mein Bruder ist ein Junge.

My brother is a boy.

bracelet
das Armband

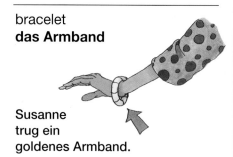

Susanne trug ein goldenes Armband.

Susan wore a gold bracelet.

braid
der Zopf

Helene liebt ihre Zöpfe.

Helen loves her braids.

branch
der Ast

Ein schwerer Ast brach von dem Baum.

A heavy branch broke off the tree.

bread
das Brot

Warmes Brot riecht sehr gut.

Warm bread smells very good.

---

break*
zerbrechen

Hast du die Glasschüssel zerbrochen?

Did you break the glass bowl?

breakfast
das Frühstück

Wir essen jeden morgen Frühstück.

We eat breakfast every morning.

breath
der Atem

Ich kann meinen Atem im Winter sehen.

I can see my breath in the winter.

breathe
atmen

Wilhelm atmet schnell wenn er rennt.

William breathes fast when he runs.

brick
der Backstein

Das Haus hat einen Kamin aus Backsteinen.

The house has a brick fireplace.

bridge
die Brücke

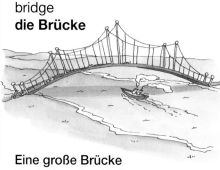

Eine große Brücke führt über den Fluß.

A long bridge goes over the river.

---

broccoli
der Broccoli

Hier ist etwas Broccoli für die Suppe.

Here is some broccoli for the soup.

broom
der Besen

Stephan kehrte den Boden mit einem Besen.

Steven swept the floor with a broom.

brother
der Bruder

Mein kleiner Bruder spielt mit mir.

My little brother plays with me.

brown
braun

Marias Hund hatte fünf braune junge Hunde.

Mary's dog had five brown puppies.

brush
bürsten

Susanne bürstet sich die Haare.

Susan is brushing her hair.

brush
die Bürste

Susanne benutzt ihre Haarbürste.

Susan is using her hair brush.

bubble
die Seifenblase

Die Badewanne ist
voller Seifenblasen.

The bathtub is full of bubbles.

bucket
der Eimer

Großvater
verschüttete einen Eimer Wasser.

Grandpa spilled a bucket of water.

buckle
die Schnalle

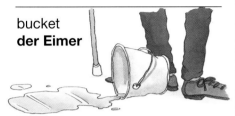

Der Gürtel
hat eine
goldene Schnalle.

The belt has a gold buckle.

buffalo
der Büffel

Büffel sind
groß und stark.

Buffalo are big and strong.

build*
bauen

Papa wird
uns ein
Baumhaus
bauen.

Dad will build us a tree house.

building
das Gebäude

Das Gebäude neben
der Kirche ist eine Schule.

The building next to the
church is a school.

bull
der Bulle

Der Bulle
stand auf der Weide.

The bull stood in the pasture.

bulletin board
**das
Anschlagbrett**

Bilder
hängen
an dem
Anschlagbrett.

Pictures hang on the bulletin board.

bun
das Brötchen

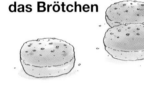

Mutter kauft Hamburger-
Brötchen in der Bäckerei.

Mom buys hamburger
buns at the bakery.

burn*
brennen

Fünf Kerzen
brennen.

Five candles are burning.

bus
der Bus

Ein Bus brachte meine
Klasse zum Museum.

A bus took my class to the museum.

bush
der Busch

Der Busch hat
neue grüne Blätter.

The bush has new green leaves.

busy
beschäftigt

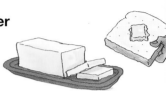

Die Biene
ist sehr
beschäftigt.

The bee is very busy.

butter
die Butter

Butter ist
gut auf Brot.

Butter is good on bread.

butterfly
der Schmetterling

Ein Schmetterling
flog über unsere Köpfe.

A butterfly flew over our heads.

button
der Knopf

Stephans Hemd
hat rote Knöpfe.

Steven's shirt has red buttons.

buy*
kaufen

Ich kaufte
einen
Ballon im Zoo.

I bought a balloon at the zoo.

by
an

Unser Hund
sitzt an dem Tor.

Our dog sits by the gate.

CcCcCcCc

cabbage
der Kohl

Kaninchen lieben Kohl.
Rabbits love cabbage.

cage
der Käfig

Ist der
Papagei
glücklich in
seinem Käfig?
Is the parrot happy in its cage?

cake
der Kuchen

Wir aßen
Schokoladenkuchen.
We ate chocolate cake.

calculator
der Taschenrechner

Addiere die
Zahlen auf dem
Taschenrechner.
Add the numbers on the calculator.

calendar
der Kalender

Der Kalender
zeigt uns
das Datum an.
The calendar
tells us the date.

calf*
das Kalb

Eine junge Kuh
wird Kalb genannt.
A baby cow is called a calf.

call
anrufen
Susanne
rief
Stephan an.
Susan called Steven.

call
der Anruf
Dieser
Telefonanruf ist für Stephan.
This telephone call is for Steven.

camel
das Kamel

Kamele
findet man in der Wüste.
Camels are found in the desert.

camp
das Lager

Im Lager haben
wir jede Nacht ein Lagerfeuer.
At camp we have a fire each night.

can
die Dose
Ich werde
eine Dose
Pfirsiche
kaufen.
I will buy a
can of peaches.

canal
der Kanal

Ein kleines Boot
fuhr durch den Kanal.
A small boat went through the canal.

candle
die Kerze

Mutter zündet
die Kerze mit
einem Streichholz an.
Mother is lighting the
candle with a match.

candy
**die Süßig-
keiten**

Die Kinder aßen
zu viele Süßigkeiten.
The children ate too much candy.

cane
der Spazierstock

Mein
Großvater
geht mit
einem
Spazierstock.
My grandpa
walks with a cane.

canoe
das Kanu

Wir gingen
auf eine Kanufahrt.
We went for a canoe ride.

cap
die Mütze

Robert
trägt
immer seine
Baseball-Mütze.
Robert always
wears his baseball cap.

car
das Auto

Dieses blaue
Auto hat neue Reifen.

This blue car has new tires.

cardinal
der Kardinal

Vor
meinem
Fenster ist ein
Kardinalvogel.

There is a cardinal
outside my window.

cards
die Karten

Wir werden nach dem
Abendessen Karten spielen.

We will play cards after dinner.

careful
vorsichtig

Der Koch ist sehr vorsichtig.

The cook is being very careful.

carpenter
der Zimmer-mann

Der Zimmermann
reparierte das Dach.

The carpenter fixed the roof.

carpet
der Teppich

Helene hat
einen neuen
Teppich in
ihrem Schlafzimmer.

Helen has a new
carpet in her bedroom.

carrot
die Möhre

Der Koch
zerschnitt
Möhren.

The cook
cut up carrots.

carry
tragen

Robert
trägt
Holz.

Robert is
carrying
wood.

cart
die Karre

Das Pferd
zog eine Heukarre.

The horse pulled a hay cart.

cartoon
die Karikatur

Susanne lachte über die Karikatur.

Susan laughed at the cartoon.

carve
schnitzen

Helene
schnitzte eine Ente aus der Seife.

Helen carved a duck from the soap.

cashier
**der Kassierer
die Kassiererin**

Wir gaben
der Kassiererin
unser Geld
für die Karten.

We gave the cashier
our money for the tickets.

cast
der Gipsver-band

Helene hat einen Gipsverband
an ihrem gebrochenen Bein.

Helen has a cast on her broken leg.

castle
das Schloß

Die Fee
hat ein
wunderschönes
Schloß.

The fairy has
a beautiful castle.

cat
die Katze

Stephans Katze schläft mit ihm.

Steven's cat sleeps with him.

catch*
fangen

Fang den
Baseball, wenn du kannst!

Catch the baseball if you can!

caterpillar
die Raupe

Bald wird
diese
Raupe ein
Schmetterling
sein.

Soon this caterpillar
will be a butterfly.

cave
die Höhle

Die Höhle ist voll
von Fledermäusen.

The cave is full of bats.

ceiling
die Decke

Die Küchendecke
ist gelb gestrichen.

The kitchen ceiling is painted yellow.

celery
der Sellerie

Helene fügte
dem Salat Sellerie zu.

Helen added celery to the salad.

cereal
das Müsli

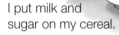

Ich tue
Milch und
Zucker auf
mein Müsli.

I put milk and
sugar on my cereal.

chair
der Stuhl

Großvater
saß auf
einem
Stuhl und
las uns vor.

Grandfather sat on
a chair and read to us.

chalk
die Kreide

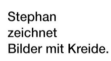

Stephan
zeichnet
Bilder mit Kreide.

Steven is drawing
pictures with chalk.

chalkboard
die Tafel

Die Lehrerin
schrieb an die Tafel.

The teacher wrote
on the chalkboard.

change
ändern

Die Blätter ändern
ihre Farben im Herbst.

Leaves change color in the fall.

change
das Kleingeld

Thomas hat
Kleingeld in
seiner Tasche.

Thomas has change in his pocket.

check
der Scheck

Ich
werde einen
Scheck in dem
Lebensmittelgeschäft schreiben.

I will write a check
at the grocery store.

checkers
das Damespiel

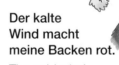

Wir spielen
Dame nach
der Schule.

We play checkers after school.

cheek
die Backe

Der kalte
Wind macht
meine Backen rot.

The cold wind
makes my cheeks red.

cheese
der Käse

Die Maus
sucht
nach Käse.

The mouse is looking for cheese.

cherry
die Kirsche

Susanne
liebt Kirschtorte.

Susan loves cherry pie.

chest
die Brust

Der junge Hund
stand auf Thomas Brust.

The puppy stood on Thomas's chest.

chick
das Kücken

Das Kücken ist weich und gelb.

The baby chick is soft and yellow.

chicken
das Huhn

Diese Hühner fressen Korn.

These chickens are eating corn.

child*
das Kind
Ein kleines Kind saß
auf dem Boden.

A small child sat
on the ground.

children
die Kinder
Zwei Kinder saßen auf der Bank.

Two children sat on the bench.

chimney
der Schornstein

Rauch kam aus dem Schornstein.

Smoke came out of the chimney.

---

chin
das Kinn

Helene hat Schokolade an ihrem Kinn.

Helen has chocolate on her chin.

---

chipmunk
das Streifenhörnchen

Streifenhörnchen haben gestreifte Rücken.

Chipmunks have striped backs.

---

chocolate
die Schokolade

Die Bäckerei verkauft Schokoladenplätzchen.

The bakery sells chocolate cookies.

---

church
die Kirche

Ich gehe mit meiner Großmutter zur Kirche.

I go to church with my grandma.

---

circle
der Kreis

Robert zeichnete zwei Kreise auf sein Papier.

Robert drew two circles on his paper.

---

circus
der Zirkus

Der Zirkus hat drei Akrobaten.

The circus has three acrobats.

---

city
die Stadt

Die Stadt hat zehn neue Gebäude.

The city has ten new buildings.

---

clap
klatschen

Das Baby wird mit dir die Hände klatschen.

The baby will clap hands with you.

---

clarinet
die Klarinette

Maria spielt Klarinette in der Kapelle.

Mary plays the clarinet in the band.

---

class
die Schulklasse

Ich habe ein Bild von meiner Schulklasse.

I have a picture of my class at school.

---

classroom
das Klassenzimmer

Unser Klassenzimmer hat viele Pulte.

Our classroom has many desks.

---

claw
die Klaue

Ein Tiger hat scharfe Klauen.

A tiger has sharp claws.

---

clay
der Lehm

Stephan machte ein Kaninchen aus Lehm.

Steven made a clay rabbit.

---

clean
putzen

Papa putzt die Fenster mit Lappen.

Dad cleans the windows with rags.

---

clean
sauber

Das Fenster ist sehr sauber.

The window is very clean.

---

clear
klar

Glas ist klar.

Glass is clear.

---

climb
hinaufsteigen

Maria steigt die Leiter hinauf.

Mary is climbing the ladder.

clock
die Uhr

Die Uhr ist in der Nähe des Bücherregals.

The clock is near the bookcase.

close
schließen

Robert schloß die Tür als er hinausging.

Robert closed the door when he went out.

close
nahe

Der Apfel steht nahe der Orange.

The apple is close to the orange.

closet
der Schrank

Mein Schrank ist voller Spielzeuge.

My closet is full of toys.

cloth
der Stoff

Tante Alice kaufte Stoff um ein Kleid zu machen.

Aunt Alice bought cloth to make a dress.

clothes
die Kleidung

Thomas Kleidung ist sehr schmutzig.

Thomas's clothes are very dirty.

clothing
die Kleidung

Die Kleidung des Babys ist blau.

The baby's clothing is blue.

cloud
die Wolke

Wolken bedeckten die Sonne.

Clouds covered the sun.

clown
der Clown

Ein Clown gab Robert eine Blume.

A clown gave Robert a flower.

coat
der Mantel

Ich trage meinen dicken Mantel wenn es schneit.

I wear my heavy coat when it snows.

cobweb
das Spinngewebe

Mein Vater machte die Spinngewebe weg.

My dad brushed away the cobwebs.

coffee
der Kaffee

Großmutter trinkt Kaffee zum Frühstück.

Grandma drinks coffee for breakfast.

coin
die Münze

Helene fand zwei Münzen in ihrer Tasche.

Helen found two coins in her pocket.

cold
kalt

Es ist zu kalt draußen zu spielen.

It is too cold to play outside.

collar
das Halsband

Der Hund trug ein ledernes Halsband.

The dog wore a leather collar.

color
die Farbe

Welche Farbe hat der Ball?

What color is the ball?

colt
das Füllen

Das Füllen läuft mit seiner Mutter.

The colt runs with its mother.

comb
der Kamm

Thomas läßt seinen Kamm auf seiner Kommode.

Thomas keeps his comb on his dresser.

come*
kommen

Komm ins Haus!
Come into the house!

comet
der Komet

Helene sah
einen Komet am Himmel.
Helen saw a comet in the sky.

comfortable
bequem

Dieses Sofa ist so sehr bequem!
This couch is so very comfortable!

compass
der Kompaß

Papa
schaute
auf seinen
Kompaß.
Dad looked at his compass.

completely
ganz

Mein Teller ist ganz sauber!
My plate is completely clean!

computer
der Computer

Wilhelm
macht
Spiele
auf seinem
Computer.
William is playing
games on his computer.

cone
die Waffel

Wir aßen
Eiscremewaffeln.
We ate ice cream cones.

contain
enthalten

Die große
Flasche
enthält
Milch.
The large bottle contains milk.

conversation
die Unterhaltung

Robert und
Susanne
führen eine
Unterhaltung.
Robert and Susan
are having a conversation.

cook
kochen
Der Koch kocht
Gemüse in einem Topf.
The cook is cooking
vegetables in a pot.

cook
der Koch
Der Koch
trägt eine weiße Schürze.
The cook is wearing a white apron.

cookie
das Plätzchen

Mama
bäckt
große
Schokoladen-
plätzchen.
Mom is baking
large chocolate cookies.

cool
kühl

Kühle
Limonade
ist gut im
Sommer.
Cool lemonade is
good in the summer.

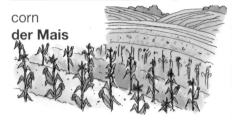

corn
der Mais

In diesem Feld wächst Mais.
Corn is growing in this field.

corner
die Ecke

Wilhelm
wartet
an der Ecke
auf den Bus.
William waits at the corner for the bus.

costume
das Kostüm

Maria trug
ein neues
Kostüm.
Mary wore a new costume.

cotton
die Baumwolle
Die
Baumwolle
für unsere
Kleidung
kommt von Pflanzen.
Cotton for our clothes
comes from plants.

cotton candy
die Zuckerwatte

Wir aßen rosa
Zuckerwatte im Zirkus.
We ate pink cotton candy at the circus.

couch
das Sofa

Papa schläft auf dem Sofa.
Dad is sleeping on the couch.

cough
husten

Bitte bedecke deinen Mund wenn du hustest!
Please cover your mouth when you cough!

cousin
der Cousin
die Cousine

Meine Cousins sind die Kinder meiner Tante.
My cousins are my aunt's children.

cover
bedecken

Großvater bedeckt die Pflanzen an kalten Nächten.
Grandpa covers the plants on cold nights.

covers
die Decken

Helene ist unter den Decken.
Helen is under the covers.

cow
die Kuh

Die Kühe schlafen nachts in der Scheune.
The cows sleep in the barn at night.

cowboy
der Cowboy

Der Cowboy legte den Sattel aufs Pferd.
The cowboy put the saddle on the horse.

coyote
der Koyote

Koyoten leben in den Bergen.
Coyotes live in the mountains.

cracker
der Kräcker

Maria nimmt Kräcker zu ihrer Suppe.
Mary adds crackers to her soup.

crane
der Kran

Ein Kran hob den Wagen.
A crane lifted the car.

crane
der Kranich

Dieser Kranich steht im Wasser.
This crane is standing in the water.

crate
die Kiste

Was ist in der Kiste?
What is in the crate?

crayon
der Buntstift

Thomas zeichnete ein Bild mit Buntstiften.
Thomas drew a picture with crayons.

cream
die Sahne

Mein Papa gießt Sahne in seinen Kaffee.
My dad puts cream in his coffee.

crocodile
das Krokodil

Wir machten ein Bild von einem Krokodil.
We took a picture of a crocodile.

crop
die Ernte

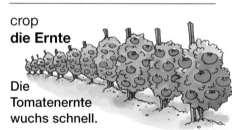

Die Tomatenernte wuchs schnell.
The crop of tomatoes grew fast.

crosswalk
der Übergang

Der Übergang ist durch weiße Streifen angezeigt.
The crosswalk is painted with white stripes.

crowd
die Menschenmenge

Eine große Menschenmenge war in dem Zirkus.
A big crowd was at the circus.

crown
die Krone

An der
Krone
der
Königin
sind Juwelen.

The queen's crown has jewels on it.

---

crush
zerdrücken

Papa zerdrückte
die Dose mit seiner Hand.

Dad crushed the can with his hand.

---

crust
die Kruste

Die Kruste ist
der beste Teil einer Torte.

The crust is the best part of a pie.

---

crutch
die Krücke

Wilhelm
geht mit
einer Krücke.

William walks with a crutch.

---

cry
weinen

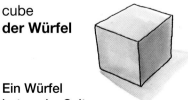

Das Kind
wird weinen
wenn seine
Flasche leer ist.

The baby will
cry if her bottle is empty.

---

cube
der Würfel

Ein Würfel
hat sechs Seiten.

A cube has six sides.

---

cucumber
die Gurke

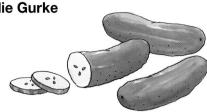

Gurken sind ein Sommergemüse.

Cucumbers are a summer vegetable.

---

cup
die Tasse

Großvater
trinkt eine
Tasse Tee
nach dem Essen.

Grandpa has a cup of tea after dinner.

---

cupboard
der Schrank

Das Geschirr wird
im Schrank aufbewahrt.

Dishes are kept in the cupboard.

---

curb
der Straßenrand

Wir
warteten
am
Straßenrand
auf den Bus.

We stood
near the curb
to wait for the bus.

---

curly
lockig

Wilhelm
hat lockiges
schwarzes Haar.

William has curly black hair.

---

curtain
der Vorhang

Die Vorhänge
wehten im Wind.

The curtains blew in the wind.

---

curve
die Kurve

Die Bergstraße hat viele Kurven.

The mountain road has many curves.

---

cut*
schneiden

Robert
schnitt
den Apfel
mit einem
scharfen Messer.

Robert cut the
apple with a sharp knife.

---

cute
niedlich

Alle Babys sind niedlich.

All babies are cute.

---

cymbal
die Zimbel

Möchtest du
gern Zimbel spielen?

Would you like to play the cymbals?

DdDdDdDd

dad
der Papa

Ich nenne meinen Vater *Papa*.

I call my father *dad*.

daisy
das Gänseblümchen

Eine Vase mit Gänse-blümchen steht auf unserem Tisch.

A vase of daisies is sitting on our table.

dance
tanzen

Maria und Wilhelm tanzen.

Mary and William are dancing.

dance
der Tanz

Maria ging mit Wilhelm zum Tanz.

Mary went to the dance with William.

dancer
der Tänzer
die Tänzerin

Die Tänzerin trug rote Schuhe.

The dancer wore red shoes.

dandelion
der Löwenzahn

In unserem Garten gibt es Löwenzahn.

There are dandelions in our yard.

dark
dunkel

Draußen ist es dunkel.

It is dark outside.

date
das Datum

Schau auf den Kalender um das Datum zu finden.

Look at the calendar to find the date.

daughter
die Tochter

Diese Frau hat zwei Töchter.

This woman has two daughters.

day
der Tag

Heute ist der Tag!

Today is the day!

deck
das Deck

Das Deck des Segelbootes ist weiß gestrichen.

The deck of the sailboat is painted white.

deep
tief

Kannst du im Tiefen des Beckens schwimmen?

Can you swim in the deep end of the pool?

deer*
das Reh

Gibt es Rehe in dem Wald?

Are there deer in the forest?

delicious
köstlich

Aprikosen sind köstlich!

Apricots are delicious!

dent
die Beule

In dieser Pfanne ist eine Beule.

There is a dent in this pan.

dentist
die Zahnarzt

Der Zahnarzt gab mir eine neue Zahnbürste.

The dentist gave me a new toothbrush.

desert
die Wüste

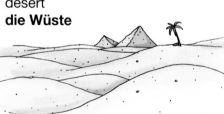

In der Wüste ist es sehr trocken.

In the desert it is very dry.

desk
das Pult

Die Lehrerin sitzt an dem Pult.

The teacher sits at the desk.

dessert
der Nachtisch

Wir essen
Eiscreme zum Nachtisch.

We are having ice cream for dessert.

dice*
die Würfel

Werfe die
Würfel um dieses Spiel zu spielen.

Throw the dice to play this game.

dictionary
das Wörterbuch

Wie viele
Bilder sind
in deinem
Wörterbuch?

How many pictures
are in your dictionary?

difficult
schwierig

Es ist
schwierig auf
den Händen
zu gehen.

It is difficult
to walk on
your hands.

dig*
graben

Thomas gräbt
im Sand nach
einem Schatz.

Thomas digs in the
sand for treasure.

dim
schwach

Das Licht
von der Kerze
war zu schwach.

The light from the
candle was too dim.

dining room
das Eßzimmer

Unser Eßzimmer hat
einen Tisch und sechs Stühle.

Our dining room has
a table and six chairs.

dinner
das Abendbrot

Wir aßen
Abendbrot
in einem Restaurant.

We ate dinner at a restaurant.

dinosaur
der Dinosaurier

Wir sahen
Dinosaurier im Museum.

We saw dinosaurs at the museum.

dirt
der Schmutz

Kehre den Schmutz
nicht unter den Teppich.

Do not sweep dirt under the rug.

dirty
schmutzig

Bitte
reinige deine
schmutzigen Schuhe!

Please clean your dirty shoes!

dishes
das Geschirr

Mein Papa
spülte das
Geschirr.

My dad washed the dishes.

dive
der Kopfsprung

Susanne
machte einen
Kopfsprung
ins Becken.

Susan took a dive into the pool.

divide
teilen

Ein
Zaun
teilt
unseren
Garten von
eurem Garten.

A fence divides
our yard from your yard.

do*
tun

Was tut sie?

What is she doing?

dock
das Dock

Die
Passagiere
warteten auf dem Dock.

The passengers waited on the dock.

doctor
der Arzt
die Ärztin

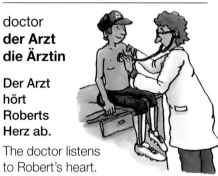

Der Arzt
hört
Roberts
Herz ab.

The doctor listens
to Robert's heart.

dog
der Hund

Wie heißt
mein Hund?

What is my dog's name?

23

doll
die Puppe

Maria hat eine Puppe mit lockigem Haar.

Mary has a doll with curly hair.

dollar
der Dollar

Ich steckte einen Dollar in meine Spardose.

I put a dollar in my bank.

dollhouse
das Puppenhaus

Das Puppenhaus hat kleine Türen und Fenster.

The dollhouse has small doors and windows.

dolphin
der Delphin

Delphine schwimmen in den Ozeanen.

Dolphins swim in the oceans.

donkey
der Esel

Robert ritt einen Esel den Berg hinauf.

Robert rode a donkey up the mountain.

door
die Tür

Großvater öffnete die Tür und sah nach draußen.

Grandpa opened the door and looked outside.

doorbell
die Türschelle

Maria läutete die Türschelle.

Mary rang the doorbell.

doorman*
der Pförtner

Der Pförtner wartet bei der Tür.

The doorman waits near the door.

dough
der Teig

Robert machte Teig für das Brot.

Robert made dough for the bread.

down
hinab

Robert fuhr auf Skiern den Hügel hinab.

Robert skied down the hill.

dozen
das Dutzend

Ein Dutzend Eier sind in einer Packung.

There are a dozen eggs in a box.

dragon
der Drache

Der Drache wohnt in einer Höhle.

The dragon lives in a cave.

draw*
zeichnen

Susanne zeichnete ein Bild von ihrem Bruder.

Susan drew a picture of her brother.

drawer
die Schublade

Die Schublade ist voller Papier und Bleistifte.

The drawer is full of paper and pencils.

dream*
träumen

Maria träumte sie wäre in einem Palast.

Mary dreamed she was in a palace.

dream
der Traum

Marias Traum machte sie glücklich.

Mary's dream made her happy.

dress
sich anziehen

Helene zieht sich für eine Party an.

Helen is dressing for a party.

dress
das Kleid

Helenes Partykleid ist rosa.

Helen's party dress is pink.

dresser
die Kommode

Meine Kommode hat fünf Schubladen.

My dresser has five drawers.

---

drink*
trinken

Ich möchte etwas Milch trinken.

I want to drink some milk.

drink
das Getränk

Milch ist ein gesundes Getränk.

Milk is a healthy drink.

---

drip
tropfen

Kaltes Wasser tropft aus dem Hahn.

Cold water drips from the faucet.

---

drive*
fahren

Wer fährt das Auto?

Who is driving the car?

---

driveway
die Einfahrt

Das Taxi wartete in der Einfahrt.

The taxi waited in the driveway.

---

drop
fallen lassen

Helene ließ ihre Bücher fallen.

Helen dropped her books.

---

drugstore
die Apotheke

Tante Alice kauft Medizin in der Apotheke.

Aunt Alice buys medicine at the drugstore.

---

drum
die Trommel

Stephan spielt Trommeln.

Steven plays the drums.

---

dry
trocken

Thomas ist trocken unter dem Schirm.

Thomas is dry under the umbrella.

---

duck
die Ente

Meine zahme Ente hat weiche weiße Federn.

My pet duck has soft, white feathers.

---

duckling
das Entchen

Die Entchen rannten hinter ihrer Mutter.

The ducklings ran behind their mother.

---

dull
langweilig

Der langweilige Film schläferte uns ein.

The dull movie put us to sleep.

---

dust
der Staub

Bringt der Staub dich zum Niesen?

Does dust make you sneeze?

---

dustpan
die Kehrschaufel

Der Besen und die Kehrschaufel sind im Schrank.

The broom and dustpan are in the closet.

E e E e E e E e

each
jede

Jede Blume ist gelb.

Each flower is yellow.

eagle
der Adler

Der Adler fliegt zu seinem Nest.

The eagle flies to its nest.

ear
das Ohr

Helene wusch
sich hinter den Ohren.
Helen washed behind her ears.

---

early
früh

Wilhelm
kam früh
zur Schule.
William came to school early.

---

earmuffs
**die
Ohrenschützer**

Robert trug
Ohrenschützer
im Schneesturm.
Robert wore earmuffs
in the snowstorm.

---

earring
der Ohrring

Meine
Mutter
trägt
lange
silberne
Ohrringe.
My mother wears
long, silver earrings.

Earth
die Erde

Wir leben auf dem Planeten Erde.
We live on the planet Earth.

---

easel
die Staffelei

Wilhelms Bild
stand auf der Staffelei.
William's picture sat on the easel.

easy
leicht

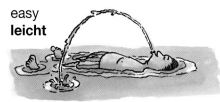

Auf meinem
Rücken dahinzutreiben ist leicht!
Floating on my back is easy!

---

eat*
essen

Wir sollen
Obst und Gemüse essen.
We should eat fruits and vegetables.

---

egg
das Ei

Großmama
wird zwei Eier kochen.
Grandma will cook two eggs.

---

elbow
der Ellbogen

Maria stieß ihren
Ellbogen am Tisch.
Mary hit her elbow on the table.

---

electricity
der Strom

Diese
Lampe
braucht
Strom.
This lamp
uses electricity.

---

elephant
der Elefant

Ein Elefant ging
in der Zirkusparade.
An elephant walked
in the circus parade.

elevator
der Aufzug

Der Aufzug
brachte
uns zum
höchsten
Stockwerk
des
Gebäudes.
The elevator
carried us
to the top
of the
building.

---

empty
leer

Eine Flasche ist leer.
One bottle is empty.

---

end
das Ende

Wo ist
das Ende
des Seils?
Where is the end of the rope?

---

engine
der Motor

Der Mechaniker
reparierte den Motor des Autos.
The mechanic fixed the car's engine.

---

entrance
der Eingang

Dieses Tor ist
der Eingang zu unserem Hof.
This gate is the entrance to our yard.

envelope
der Umschlag

Leck den Umschlag um ihn zu schließen.

Lick the envelope to close it.

---

equator
der Äquator

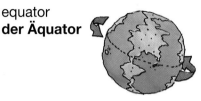

Der Äquator geht um die Erde.

The equator goes around the Earth.

---

erase
abwischen

Helene wischt die Tafel ab.

Helen is erasing the blackboard.

---

eraser
das Radiergummi

Stephan kaufte Bleistifte mit großen Radiergummis.

Steven bought pencils with large erasers.

---

evening
der Abend

Die Sonne geht am Abend unter.

The sun goes down in the evening.

---

every
jedes

Jedes Kind lächelte.

Every child smiled.

---

exam
das Examen

Maria schreibt ein Examen.

Mary is taking an exam.

---

eye
das Auge

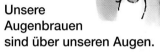

Meine Augen sind blau.

My eyes are blue.

---

eyebrow
die Augenbraue

Unsere Augenbrauen sind über unseren Augen.

Our eyebrows are above our eyes.

F f F f F f F f

face
das Gesicht

Bitte bring ein Lächeln in dein Gesicht!

Please put a smile on your face!

---

factory
die Fabrik

Diese Fabrik macht Autos.

This factory makes cars.

---

fairy
Fee

Die Fee gab der Königin einige Juwelen.

The fairy gave the queen some jewels.

---

fall*
fallen

Jimmy fällt hin.

Jimmy falls down.

---

fall
der Herbst

Meine Familie harkt Blätter im Herbst.

My family rakes leaves in the fall.

---

family
die Familie

Das ist ein Bild von meiner Familie.

This is a picture of my family.

---

fan
der Ventilator

Helene sitzt nahe beim Ventilator wenn ihr heiß ist.

Helen sits near the fan when she is hot.

---

far
weit

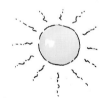

Die Sonne ist weit von der Erde.

The sun is far from the Earth.

farm
der Bauernhof

Hühner, Kühe, und Schweine leben auf dem Bauernhof.

Chickens, cows, and pigs live on the farm.

farmer
der Bauer

Der Bauer pflanzt Mais.

The farmer is planting corn.

fast
schnell

Die Rennwagen fahren schnell vorbei.

The race cars go by fast.

fat
dick

Der Weihnachts-mann ist dick.

Santa Claus is fat.

father
der Vater

Dieser Vater hat viele Kinder.

This father has many children.

faucet
der Wasserhahn

Heißes und kaltes Wasser kommen aus dem Wasserhahn.

Hot and cold water come from the faucet.

favorite
am liebsten

Schokolade habe ich am liebsten.

Chocolate is my favorite.

feather
die Feder

Vögel sind mit Federn bedeckt.

Birds are covered with feathers.

feet*
die Füße

Der Sand war heiß auf Helenes Füßen.

The sand was hot on Helen's feet.

fence
der Zaun

Wilhelm baut einen Zaun um den Garten.

William is building a fence around the garden.

fern
der Farn

Farne sind grüne Pflanzen.

Ferns are green plants.

fever
das Fieber

Wie hoch ist Stephans Fieber?

How high is Steven's fever?

field
das Feld

Die Kühe sind auf dem Feld.

The cows are in the field.

fill
füllen

Großmutter füllt die Gläser bis an den Rand.

Grandma fills the glasses to the top.

fin
die Flosse

Fische schwimmen mit ihren Flossen.

Fish swim with their fins.

find*
finden

Hier finden wir den Schatz!

We will find the treasure here!

finger
der Finger

Meine Finger werden im Winter kalt.

My fingers become cold in the winter.

fingernail
der Fingernagel

Tante Alice malte ihre Fingernägel rot.

Aunt Alice painted her fingernails red.

fire
das Feuer

Onkel Eduard steckte das Feuer mit einem Streichholz an.

Uncle Edward lit the fire with a match.

---

fire engine
die Feuerwehr

Die Feuerwehr raste zum Feuer.

The fire engine raced to the fire.

---

fire fighter
der Feuerwehrmann

Ein Feuerwehrmann trägt einen Hut, einen Regenmantel und Stiefel.

A fire fighter wears a hat, a raincoat, and boots.

---

fireplace
der Kamin

Dieses Haus hat einen Kamin im Wohnzimmer.

This house has a fireplace in the living room.

---

first
zuerst

Thomas kommt zuerst.

Thomas is first in line.

---

fish*
der Fisch

Großvater möchte Fisch zum Abendessen.

Grandpa wants fish for dinner.

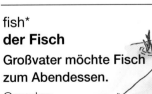

fish
fischen

Großvater fischt am See.

Grandpa is fishing at the lake.

---

fisherman*
der Fischer

Der Fischer fing zwei Fische.

The fisherman caught two fish.

---

fix
reparieren

Helene wird das zerbrochene Spielzeug reparieren.

Helen will fix the broken toy.

---

flag
die Fahne

Helene trug die Fahne in der Parade.

Helen carried the flag in the parade.

---

flame
die Flamme

Die Kerzenflamme ist gelb.

The candle flame is yellow.

---

flamingo
der Flamingo

Ein Flamingo hat lange Beine.

A flamingo has long legs.

---

flashlight
die Taschenlampe

Maria trug eine Taschenlampe um im Dunkeln zu sehen.

Mary carried a flashlight to see in the dark.

---

flat
flach

Papier ist flach.

Paper is flat.

---

flavor
der Geschmack

Welchen Geschmack hast du bei Eiscreme gern?

What flavor of ice cream do you like?

---

float
schweben

Der Ballon des kleinen Mädchens schwebte davon.

The little girl's balloons floated away.

---

floor
der Fußboden

Der Schlafzimmerfußboden ist mit Kleidern bedeckt.

The bedroom floor is covered with clothes.

---

florist
der Blumenhändler

Ein Blumenhändler verkauft Blumen und Pflanzen.

A florist sells flowers and plants.

---

flour
das Mehl

Der Koch fügt dem Plätzchenteig Mehl zu.

The cook adds flour to the cookie dough.

flower
die Blume

Sind diese
Blumen orange?

Are these flowers orange?

flowerbed
das Blumenbeet

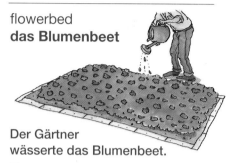

Der Gärtner
wässerte das Blumenbeet.

The gardener watered the flowerbed.

flu
die Grippe

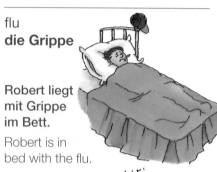

Robert liegt
mit Grippe
im Bett.

Robert is in
bed with the flu.

flute
die Flöte

Stephan
spielt Flöte im Orchester.

Steven plays the flute in the orchestra.

fly*
fliegen

Das
Flugzeug
fliegt über der Stadt.

The airplane is flying over the town.

fly
die Fliege

Eine
Fliege
fliegt um das
Essen herum.

A fly flies around the food.

fog
der Nebel

Grauer
Nebel bedeckt die Stadt.

Gray fog covers the city.

follow
folgen

Die Katze folgte mir nach Hause.

The cat followed me home.

food
das Essen

Das Essen steht auf dem Tisch.

The food is on the table.

foolish
dumm

Es ist dumm,
mit Streich-
hölzern zu
spielen.

Playing with matches is foolish.

foot*
der Fuß

Das Baby
spielte mit seinem Fuß.

The baby played with his foot.

football
das Fußballspiel

Robert
spielt Fußball.

Robert plays football.

footprint
die Fußspur

Unsere Fußspuren zeichnen
sich im nassen Sand ab.

Our footprints show in the wet sand.

footstool
die Fußbank

Das kleine
Mädchen
saß auf
einer
Fußbank.

The little girl
sat on a footstool.

for
zu

Wir essen
Truthahn zu dem Abendessen.

We are having turkey for dinner.

forehead
die Stirn

Meine Stirn
ist über meinen Augenbrauen.

My forehead is above my eyebrows.

forest
der Wald

Der Wald ist voller Bäume.

The forest is full of trees.

forget*
vergessen

Susanne
vergißt immer ihre Brille.

Susan always forgets her glasses.

fork
die Gabel

Maria aß ihren Salat mit einer Gabel.

Mary ate her salad with a fork.

fountain
der Springbrunnen

Im Park ist ein Springbrunnen.

There is a fountain in the park.

fox
der Fuchs

Der Fuchs rannte durch den Garten.

The fox ran through the yard.

freckles
die Sommer-sprossen

Robert hat Sommersprossen auf seiner Nase.

Robert has freckles on his nose.

freeze*
frieren

Im Winter friert Wasser zu Eis.

Water freezes into ice in the winter.

freezer
die Gefriertruhe

In unserer Gefriertruhe ist Eiscreme.

Our freezer has ice cream in it.

french fries
die Pommes Frites

Stephan aß Pommes Frites zu seinem Hamburger.

Steven ate french fries with his hamburger.

friend
**der Freund
die Freundin**

Mein Freund spielt gern Ball.

My friend likes to play ball.

frog
der Frosch

Ein Frosch sprang in den Teich.

A frog jumped into the pond.

from
von

Saft kommt von Früchten.

Juice comes from fruit.

frost
der Frost

Wir sahen heute morgen Frost auf dem Rasen.

We saw frost on the lawn this morning.

fruit
das Obst

Helene hatte etwas Obst als Imbiß.

Helen had some fruit for a snack.

full
voll

Helenes Teller ist voll mit Essen.

Helen's plate is full of food.

fun
der Spaß

Geburtstagspartys machen soviel Spaß!

Birthday parties are so much fun!

funnel
der Trichter

Papa goß das Öl mit einem Trichter ins Auto.

Dad put the oil in the car with a funnel.

fur
der Pelz

Der Wolf hat einen dicken Pelz.

The wolf has heavy fur.

furnace
die Heizung

Die Heizung macht unser Haus warm.

The furnace makes our house warm.

furniture
die Möbel

Großvaters alte Möbel sind in der Dachstube.

Grandpa's old furniture is in the attic.

GgGgGgGg

game
das Spiel

Maria und ihre Schwester
spielen nach der Schule Spiele.

Mary and her sister
play games after school.

garage
die Garage

Wir haben
unser Auto in der Garage.

We keep our car in the garage.

garden
der Garten

Thomas pflanzte
Blumen in seinem Garten.

Thomas planted flowers in his garden.

gardener
der Gärtner

Ein
Gärtner muß
Unkraut herausziehen.

A gardener must pull weeds.

garden hose
der Gartenschlauch

Thomas
wässert die
Pflanzen mit dem Gartenschlauch.

Thomas waters the
plants with the garden hose.

gas
das Gas

Unser Ofen
benutzt Gas.

Our stove uses gas.

gasoline
das Benzin

Unser
Rasenmäher läuft mit Benzin.

The lawn mower runs on gasoline.

gate
das Tor

Wilhelm
öffnete das
Tor in dem Zaun.

William opened
the gate in the fence.

ghost
der Geist

Es gibt nicht
so etwas
wie einen Geist.

There is no such thing as a ghost.

gift
das Geschenk

Ich brachte
ein Geschenk
zur Geburtstagsparty.

I took a gift to the birthday party.

gills
die Kiemen

Kiemen helfen
den Fischen im
Wasser zu atmen.

Gills help fish breathe in the water.

giraffe
die Giraffe

Die Giraffe
ist ein
sehr
großes
Tier.

The giraffe
is a very
tall animal.

girl
das Mädchen

Meine
Schwester
ist ein
Mädchen.

My sister is a girl.

give*
geben

Gib deinem Bruder die Schachtel.

Give the box to your brother.

glad
froh

Wir sind froh, daß du zum
Abendessen gekommen bist.

We are glad you came for dinner.

glass
das Glas

Großvater
füllte das
Glas mit Milch.

Grandfather filled
the glass with milk.

glass
das Glas

Das
Fenster ist aus Glas gemacht.

The window is made of glass.

glasses
die Brille

Wilhelm trägt eine Brille um zu sehen.

William wears glasses to help him see.

---

globe
der Globus

Ein Globus steht auf dem Pult des Lehrers.

A globe sits on the teacher's desk.

---

glove
der Handschuh

Handschuhe halten unsere Hände im Winter warm.

Gloves keep our hands warm in the winter.

---

glue
leimen

Wer leimte die Tasse zusammen?

Who glued the cup together?

glue
der Leim

Wer hat den Leim auf den Tisch tropfen gelassen?

Who spilled glue on the table?

---

go*
gehen

Wir werden zur Schule gehen.

We will go to school.

---

goat
die Ziege

Ziegen essen viele Dinge!

Goats eat many things!

---

goggles
die Schutzbrille

Helene trägt eine Schutzbrille unter Wasser.

Helen wears goggles under the water.

---

gold
golden

Der Mann hat eine goldene Uhr.

The man has a gold watch.

---

good*
gut

Das Wetter ist gut um in dem Park zu spielen.

The weather is good for playing in the park.

---

goose*
die Gans

Susanne hat eine zahme Gans.

Susan has a pet goose.

---

gorilla
der Gorilla

Der Gorilla im Zoo frißt Obst und Gemüse.

The gorilla at the zoo eats fruits and vegetables.

---

gosling
das Gänschen

Ein Gänschen ist eine junge Gans.

A gosling is a baby goose.

---

grandfather
der Großvater

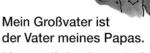

Mein Großvater ist der Vater meines Papas.

My grandfather is my dad's father.

---

grandmother
die Großmutter

Meine Großmutter ist die Mutter meines Papas.

My grandmother is my dad's mother.

---

grandpa
der Großpapa

Großpapa liest mir ein Buch vor.

Grandpa reads a book to me.

---

grandparents
die Großeltern

Großeltern sind die Eltern unserer Eltern.

Grandparents are the parents of our parents.

---

grape
die Traube

Trauben sind grün oder purpur.

Grapes are green or purple.

---

grapefruit
die Pampelmuse

Thomas aß Pampelmuse zum Mittagessen.

Thomas ate grapefruit for lunch.

grass
das Gras

Das Gras
im Hof ist zu hoch.

The grass in the yard is too tall.

grasshopper
die Heuschrecke

Heuschrecken haben Flügel.

Grasshoppers have wings.

gravy
die Soße

Maria
tat
Soße
auf ihre
Kartoffeln.

Mary put gravy on her potatoes.

gray
grau

Thomas
Papagei ist grau.

Thomas's parrot is gray.

green
grün

Das Gras ist grün.

The grass is green.

greenhouse
das Gewächs-haus

Ein
Gewächshaus
ist ein gläsernes
Haus für Pflanzen.

A greenhouse is
a glass house for plants.

grocery store
das Lebensmittelgeschäft

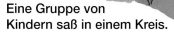

Großpapa
kaufte einen
Fisch im
Lebensmittelgeschäft.

Grandpa bought a fish
at the grocery store.

ground
der Boden

Stephan
saß auf
dem Boden
und dachte nach.

Steven sat on the ground and thought.

group
die Gruppe

Eine Gruppe von
Kindern saß in einem Kreis.

A group of children sat in a circle.

grow*
wachsen

Jimmy
wächst
rasch.

Jimmy is
growing fast.

guest
der Gast

Unsere
Gäste
klingelten.

Our guests
rang the doorbell.

guitar
die Gitarre

Wilhelm
spielt Gitarre.

William plays the guitar.

HhHhHhHh

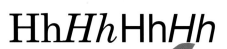

hair
das Haar

Wilhelm bürstet
sich die Haare.

William is brushing his hair.

half*
halb

Maria
aß die
halbe Melone.

Mary ate half the melon.

ham
der Schinken

Wir hatten Schinken
zum Abendessen.

We had ham for dinner.

hamburger
der Hamburger

Ich aß einen
Hamburger zum Abendessen.

I had a hamburger for dinner.

hammer
hämmern

Thomas hämmerte den
Nagel in das Holz.

Thomas hammered
the nail into
the wood.

hammer
der Hammer

Thomas schlug den
Nagel mit einem Hammer.

Thomas hit the nail with a hammer.

hammock
die Hängematte

Robert
schläft in einer Hängematte.

Robert sleeps in a hammock.

hand
die Hand

Stephan wusch
seine Hände.

Steven washed his hands.

handkerchief*
das Taschentuch

Thomas
trägt
immer ein
Taschentuch.

Thomas always
carries a handkerchief.

handsome
gutaussehend

Der Schau-
spieler war sehr gutaussehend.

The actor was very handsome.

hang*
hängen

Maria
hängt
ihren
Mantel
hinter
die Tür.

Mary hangs
her coat
behind the door.

hanger
der Kleiderbügel

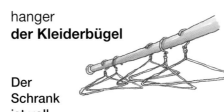

Der
Schrank
ist voll
leerer Kleiderbügel.

The closet is full of empty hangers.

happy
glücklich

Leute
lächeln wenn
sie glücklich sind.

People smile when they are happy.

hard
schwierig

Es ist
schwierig
auf den
Händen
zu gehen.

It is hard
to walk on
your hands.

hard
hart

Der
Fußboden
ist hart!

The floor is hard!

harp
die Harfe

Eine Harfe
hat viele
Saiten.

A harp has
many strings.

hat
der Hut

Meine Tante
trägt immer
einen Hut
zur Kirche.

My aunt always
wears a hat to church.

have*
haben

Sie haben rote Hüte.

They have red hats.

hay
das Heu

Pferde und Kühe fressen Heu.

Horses and cows eat hay.

head
der Kopf

Der Papagei
saß auf meinem Kopf!

The parrot sat on my head!

healthy
gesund

Stephan
und Helene
sehen sehr gesund aus.

Steven and Helen look very healthy.

heart
das Herz

Mein Herz
ist genau hier.

My heart is right here.

heat
die Hitze

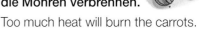

Zu viel Hitze wird
die Möhren verbrennen.

Too much heat will burn the carrots.

heavy
schwer

Der Kasten ist zu schwer zu heben.

The box is too heavy to lift.

---

helicopter
der Hubschrauber

Ein Hubschrauber flog über unser Haus.

A helicopter flew over our house.

---

help
helfen

Tante Alice hilft Jimmy aufzustehen.

Aunt Alice helps Jimmy stand up.

---

hen
die Henne

Die Henne bewachte ihre Kücken.

The hen watched her chicks.

---

herd
die Herde

Eine Herde Schafe ging auf der Straße.

A herd of sheep walked on the road.

---

here
hierhin

Stell es hierhin bitte.

Put it here, please.

---

high
hoch

Die Plätzchen sind auf einem hohen Regal.

The cookies are on a high shelf.

---

hill
der Hügel

Das Hündchen rannte den Hügel hinauf.

The puppy ran up the hill.

---

hippopotamus
das Nilpferd

Ein Nilpferd ging in den Fluß.

A hippopotamus walked into the river.

---

hit*
schlagen

Robert schlug den Baseball in das Feld.

Robert hit the baseball into the field.

---

hockey
das Hockeyspiel

Hockey wird auf Schlittschuhen gespielt.

Hockey is played on ice skates.

---

hoe
hacken

Maria hackte oft ihren Garten.

Mary hoed her garden often.

---

hoe
die Hacke

Thomas benutzte seine Hacke um seinen Garten zu jäten.

Thomas used his hoe to weed his garden.

---

hold*
halten

Ich kann das Kätzchen in meiner Hand halten.

I can hold the kitten in my hand.

---

hole
das Loch

Der Hund gräbt ein Loch für seinen Knochen.

The dog is digging a hole for its bone.

---

home
das Heim

Dein Heim ist wo du deinen Hut aufhängst.

Home is where you hang your hat.

---

homework
die Hausaufgabe

Stephan hat keine Hausaufgaben mehr zu tun!

Steven has no more homework to do!

---

honey
der Honig

Bären lieben Honig.

Bears love honey.

hood
die Kapuze

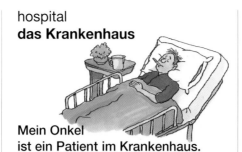

Helenes Wintermantel hat eine Kapuze.

Helen's winter coat has a hood.

hoof*
der Huf

Der Huf des Pferdes hat ein neues Hufeisen.

The horse's hoof has a new shoe.

hoop
der Reifen

Der Zirkushund sprang durch den Reifen.

The circus dog jumped through the hoop.

horn
das Horn

Manche Tiere haben Hörner.

Many animals have horns.

horse
das Pferd

Thomas reitet sein Pferd auf der Ranch.

Thomas rides his horse on the ranch.

hose
der Schlauch

Susanne benutzte den Schlauch, um den Garten zu wässern.

Susan used the hose to water the garden.

---

hospital
das Krankenhaus

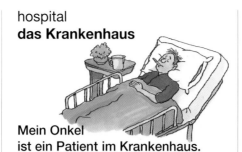

Mein Onkel ist ein Patient im Krankenhaus.

My uncle is a patient at the hospital.

hot
heiß

Es ist heiß im Sommer.

It is hot in the summer.

hotel
das Hotel

Wir schliefen eine Nacht in einem Hotel.

We slept in a hotel for a night.

hour
die Stunde

Maria machte ihre Hausaufgaben in einer Stunde.

Mary did her homework in an hour.

house
das Haus

Stephan wohnt in einem Haus an einer Ecke.

Steven lives in a house on a corner.

how
wie

Wie heiß ist es?

How hot is it?

---

hug
umarmen

Meine Mama umarmt mich wenn sie glücklich ist.

My mom hugs me when she is happy.

hump
der Höcker

Kamele haben Höcker auf ihren Rücken.

Camels have humps on their backs.

hungry
hungrig

Der Hund ist sehr hungrig.

The dog is very hungry.

hunt
suchen...nach

Helene sucht nach ihren Schuhen.

Helen is hunting for her shoes.

hurt*
verletzen

Helene stieß sich an der Tür und verletzte ihren Kopf.

Helen ran into the door and hurt her head.

I i *I i* I i *I i*

ice
das Eis

Beim
kalten
Wetter
gefriert
Wasser zu Eis.
In cold weather,
water freezes into ice.

ice cream
die Eiscreme

Eiscreme
schmilzt
schnell
im Sommer.
Ice cream melts
fast in the summer.

ice skate
der Schlittschuh

Diese neuen
Schlittschuhe
sind für
Roberts Geburtstag.
These new ice skates
are for Robert's birthday.

icicle
der Eiszapfen

Eiszapfen
hängen im
Winter
vom Dach.
Icicles hang from
the roof in winter.

in front of
vor

Der
Briefkasten
steht vor
dem Haus.
The mailbox is in front of the house.

ink
die Tinte

Thomas Füllhalter
verwendet schwarze Tinte.
Thomas's pen uses black ink.

insect
das Insekt

Heuschrecken
und Fliegen
sind Insekten.
Grasshoppers and flies are insects.

into
in

Leg die
Banane in
den Lunchbeutel.
Put the banana into the lunch bag.

iron
das Bügeleisen

Vorsicht! Das
Bügeleisen ist heiß.
Careful—the iron is hot!

island
die
Insel

Eine
Insel ist von Wasser umgegeben.
An island is surrounded by water.

J j *J j* J j *J j*

jacket
die Jacke

Robert trägt
eine Jacke im Frühling.
Robert wears a jacket in the spring.

jam
die Marmelade

Maria
liebt Toast mit Marmelade.
Mary loves toast with jam.

jeans
die Jeans

Robert trägt alte
Jeans um den Boden zu reinigen.
Robert wears old
jeans to clean the floor.

Jeep
der Jeep

Der Jeep
fuhr die
Bergstraße
hinauf.
The Jeep drove
up the mountain road.

jelly
das Gelee

Manche Kuchen
enthalten Gelee.
Some cakes have jelly in them.

jet
der Jet

Bist du schon mit
einem Jet geflogen?

Have you flown on a jet?

jewel
das Juwel

Ihr
Halsband
hat viele
Juwelen.

Her necklace has many jewels on it.

jeweler
der Juwelier

Der Juwelier verkauft
Ringe und Armbänder.

The jeweler sells rings and bracelets.

jigsaw puzzle
das Puzzlespiel

Robert setzte ein
Puzzlespiel zusammen.

Robert put together a jigsaw puzzle.

jog
joggen

Stephan und sein
Papa joggen im Park.

Steven and his dad jog in the park.

juggle
jonglieren

Wie
viele
Bälle
jongliert
der Clown?

How many balls is
the clown juggling?

juice
der Saft

Jimmy
möchte Saft.

Jimmy wants juice.

jump
springen

Maria kann über
den Zaun springen.

Mary can jump over the fence.

jungle
der Dschungel

Es ist sehr
heiß im Dschungel.

It is very hot in the jungle.

jungle gym
das Klettergerüst

Die Kinder
klettern auf
dem Klettergerüst.

The children climb
on the jungle gym.

KkKkKkKk

kangaroo
das Känguruh

Ein Känguruh kann
sehr weit springen.

A kangaroo can jump very far.

keep*
behalten

Stephans Mama
behält alle seine Examen.

Steven's mom keeps all his exams.

ketchup
das Ketchup

Helene tat
Ketchup auf
ihren Hamburger.

Helen put ketchup on her hamburger.

kettle
der Kessel

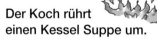

Der Koch rührt
einen Kessel Suppe um.

The cook is stirring a kettle of soup.

key
der Schlüssel

Die Tür kann
mit diesem
Schlüssel
geöffnet werden.

The door can be
opened with this key.

kick
der Tritt

Robert gab dem Ball einen harten Tritt.

Robert gave the ball a hard kick.

kick
treten

Robert trat den Fußball.

Robert kicked the football.

kid
das Zicklein

Ein Zicklein ist eine junge Ziege.

A kid is a baby goat.

king
der König

Der König wohnt in einem Schloß.

The king lives in a castle.

kitchen
die Küche

Wir essen in der Küche.

We eat in the kitchen.

kite
der Drache

Thomas Drache ist hoch am Himmel.

Thomas's kite is high in the sky.

kitten
das Kätzchen

Meine Katze ist ihren Kätzchen eine gute Mutter.

My cat is a good mother to her kittens.

knee
das Knie

Stephan verletzte sein Knie beim Fußballspielen.

Steven hurt his knee playing football.

knife*
das Messer

Maria ließ ihr Messer auf den Boden fallen.

Mary dropped her knife on the floor.

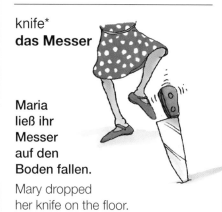

knit*
stricken

Großmutter strickte ihrem Hund einen Sweater.

Grandma knit her dog a sweater.

knot
der Knoten

Susanne band ihre Schuhriemen zu Knoten.

Susan tied her shoelaces in knots.

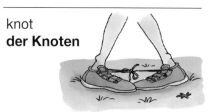

Ll Ll Ll Ll

label
das Etikett

Robert las das Etikett auf der Suppendose.

Robert read the label on the soup can.

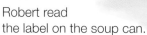

lace
die Spitze

Unsere Vorhänge sind aus Spitze gemacht.

Our curtains are made of lace.

ladder
die Leiter

Der Feuerwehrmann kletterte auf einer Leiter aufs Dach.

The fire fighter climbed a ladder to the roof.

lake
der See

Wir fischen und schwimmen gern im See.

We like to fish and swim at the lake.

lamb
das Lamm

Die Lämmer spielen gerne.

The lambs love to play.

lamp
die Lampe

Eine große Lampe beleuchtet das Schlafzimmer.

A large lamp lights up the bedroom.

lap
der Schoß

Wenn ich mich setze springt mir meine Katze auf den Schoß.

When I sit down, my cat jumps up on my lap.

large
groß

Die Jacke ist zu groß für Maria.

The jacket is too large for Mary.

last
letzt

Wer möchte das letzte Stück Kuchen?

Who wants the last piece of cake?

late
spät

Mama kam zu spät zur Arbeit.

Mom was late for work.

laugh
lachen

Susanne lacht über den Clown.

Susan is laughing at the clown.

laugh
das Lachen

Susannes Lachen ist sehr laut.

Susan's laugh is very loud.

laundry
die Wäsche

Dieser Haufen Wäsche muß gewaschen werden.

This pile of laundry has to be washed.

lawn
der Rasen

Thomas saß auf dem Rasen unter einem Baum.

Thomas sat on the lawn under a tree.

lawn mower
der Rasen-mäher

Papa mähte das Gras mit dem Rasenmäher.

Dad cut the grass with the lawn mower.

lazy
faul

Maria war faul und wollte ihr Zimmer nicht putzen.

Mary was lazy and would not clean her room.

leaf*
das Blatt

Ein Blatt fiel von dem Baum in meinen Schoß.

A leaf fell off the tree into my lap.

leap*
springen

Es macht Spaß im Regen über Pfützen zu springen.

It's fun to leap over puddles in the rain.

learn
lernen

In der Schule lernen wir lesen.

At school we are learning to read.

leather
das Leder

Roberts Schuhe sind aus Leder.

Robert's shoes are leather.

leave*
verlassen

Nach dem Frühstuck verlasse ich das Haus um in die Schule zu gehen.

I leave the house for school after breakfast.

left
link

Wilhelm hielt den Ballon in seiner linken Hand.

William held the balloon in his left hand.

leg
das Bein

Die Spinne
hat sehr lange Beine.

The spider has very long legs.

lemon
die Zitrone

Helene drückt Zitronen aus.

Helen is squeezing lemons.

lemonade
die Limonade

Wir trinken
Limonade, wenn
das Wetter heiß ist.

We drink lemonade
when the weather is hot.

leopard
der Leopard

Ein Leopard lebt im Zoo.

A leopard lives at the zoo.

less*
weniger

Robert
hat weniger
Nachtisch
als Susanne.

Robert has less
dessert than Susan does.

lesson
der Unterricht

Es ist Zeit
für Helenes
Geigenunterricht.

It is time for Helen's violin lesson.

letter
der Brief

Wirst du
mir einen Brief schreiben?

Will you write me a letter?

letter carrier
der Briefträger

Der Briefträger
füllt unseren Briefkasten.

The letter carrier fills our mailbox.

lettuce
der Blattsalat

Wilhelm tat
Blattsalat
in den Salat.

William put
lettuce in the salad.

librarian
**der Bibliothekar
die Bibliothekarin**

Die Bibliothekarin
hilft mir Bücher zu finden.

The librarian helps me find books.

lick
lecken

Maria
leckt ihre
Eiswaffel.

Mary is licking
her ice cream cone.

lift
heben

Bitte hebe
den Deckel
des Kastens auf.

Please lift the top of the box.

light*
anzünden

Mutter zündet eine Kerze an.

Mother is lighting a candle.

lightbulb
die Glühbirne

Maria tat eine
neue Glühbirne in die Lampe.

Mary put a new lightbulb in the lamp.

lightning
der Blitz

Der Blitz
erhellt den
Nachthimmel.

Lightning lights up the night sky.

like
wie

Eine ist wie die andere.

One is like the other.

like
mögen

Stephan mag Eiscreme!

Steven likes ice cream!

lime
die Limone

Welche Farbe hat die Limone?

What color is the lime?

line
die Reihe

Ich stehe nicht
gerne in der Reihe.

I do not like standing in line.

lion
der Löwe

Die
Löwen schlafen.

The lions are sleeping.

lip
die Lippe

Helene biß
ihre Lippe.

Helen bit her lip.

list
die Liste

Wie viele
Dinge stehen
auf der Liste?

How many things are on the list?

listen
anhören

Die Studenten
hören die Musik an.

The students listen to the music.

little
klein

Die Schuhe des
Babys sind klein.

The baby's shoes are little.

live
wohnen

Der Hund
wohnt in einem kleinen Haus.

The dog lives in a small house.

living room
das Wohnzimmer

Unser Wohnzimmer
hat einen Kamin.

Our living room has a fireplace.

lizard
die Eidechse

Eine Eidechse saß
auf einem Stein im Sonnenlicht.

A lizard sat on a rock in the sun.

lobster
der Hummer

Der
Fischer fing
einen Hummer.

The fisherman caught a lobster.

lock
abschließen

Helene schloß die
Tür ab als
sie ausging.

Helen locked
the door
when she left.

lock
das Schloß

Zwei Schlösser
sind an der Tür.

There are two locks on the door.

log
das Holzscheit

Onkel
Eduard
trug ein Paar
Holzscheite herein.

Uncle Edward
carried in some logs.

lollipop
der Lutscher

Jimmy
ließ seinen
Lutscher fallen.

Jimmy dropped his lollipop.

long
lang

Die Hosen
sind zu lang
für Thomas.

The pants are
too long for Thomas.

look
sehen

Helene
sieht auf die Kirschtorte.

Helen is looking at the cherry pie.

loud
laut

Die Glocke
ist sehr laut!

The bell is very loud!

love
lieben

Mama liebt
Jimmy sehr.

Mommy loves Jimmy very much.

lunch
das Mittagessen

Wir aßen Suppe
und belegte Brote
zum Mittagessen.

We ate soup
and sandwiches for lunch.

Mm*Mm* Mm*Mm*

magazine
die Zeitschrift

Thomas liest
Zeitschriften
zu Hause.
Thomas reads
magazines at home.

magician
der Zauberer

Der Zauberer
zog ein
Kaninchen
aus
seinem Hut.
The magician
pulled a rabbit
out of his hat.

magnet
der Magnet

Die Nägel
werden von
einem Magnet angezogen.

The nails are pulled by a magnet.

mail
die Post

Mit der
Post
kam ein
Brief für
Susanne.
A letter came for Susan in the mail.

mailbox
der Briefkasten

Jedes Haus hat
einen Briefkasten.
Every home has a mailbox.

make*
machen

Helene machte
eine Torte zum Nachtisch.
Helen made a pie for dessert.

make-believe
die Phantasie

Kinder machen Phantasiespiele.
Children play make-believe.

man*
der Mann

Mein Onkel
ist ein großer
Mann.
My uncle is
a tall man.

mane
die Mähne

Das Pferd
hat eine lange Mähne.
The horse has a long mane.

many
viele

Zu viele Kerzen!
Too many candles!

map
die Landkarte

Roberts Landkarte zeigt die Stadt.
Robert's map shows the city.

mask
die Maske

Das Kostüm
hat eine blöde Maske.
The costume has a silly mask.

match
das Streichholz

Papa zündete
das Feuer mit
seinen Streichhölzern an.
Dad lit the fire with his matches.

match
zusammen passen

Diese
Socken passen
nicht zusammen.
These socks do not match.

meal
das Mahl

Das
Frühstück
ist das Morgenmahl.
Breakfast is the morning meal.

meat
das Fleisch

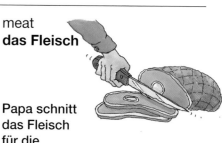

Papa schnitt
das Fleisch
für die
belegten Brote.
Dad cut up the
meat for sandwiches.

mechanic
der Mechaniker

Ein
Mechaniker
repariert
Autos in der
Tankstelle.

A mechanic fixes
cars at the gas station.

---

medal
die Medaille

Der Läufer
gewann eine
Medaille.

The runner
won a medal.

---

medicine
die Medizin

Roberts
Mutter
gab ihm
etwas Medizin.

Robert's mother
gave him some medicine.

---

medium
mittelgroß

Mittelgroß ist
zwischen groß und klein.

Medium is between large and small.

---

melon
die Melone

Großvater
pflanzte Melonen
in seinem Garten.

Grandfather planted
melons in his garden.

---

melt
schmelzen

Helenes
Eiscreme schmolz.

Helen's ice cream melted.

---

menu
**die
Speisekarte**

Ich las
die Speisekarte im Restaurant.

I read the menu at the restaurant.

---

messy
schmutzig

Thomas Gesicht
ist schmutzig.

Thomas's face is messy.

---

microphone
das Mikrofon

Der Sänger
sang in
ein Mikrofon.

The singer sang
into a microphone.

---

microscope
das Mikroskop

Das
Mikroskop
läßt kleine
Sachen groß
erscheinen.

The microscope
makes small things look big.

---

milk
die Milch

Milch gibt
einem starke
Knochen
und Zähne.

Milk gives you strong
bones and teeth.

---

mirror
der Spiegel

Helene
betrachtet sich
im Spiegel.

Helen is looking at
herself in the mirror.

---

mittens
**die Faust-
handschuhe**

Robert
trägt seine
Faust-
handschuhe
draußen im
Schnee.

Robert wears his
mittens outside in the snow.

---

mix
mischen

Wilhelm
mischte
Mehl in den
Plätzchenteig.

William mixed flour
into the cookie dough.

---

mom
die Mama

Ich nenne meine Mutter *Mama*.

I call my mother *mom*.

---

money
das Geld

Robert
kaufte einen
Ball mit seinem Geld.

Robert bought a ball with his money.

---

monkey
der Affe

Der Affe
sprang von
Ast zu Ast.

The monkey jumped
from branch to branch.

month
der Monat

Ein Monat hat vier Wochen.
There are four weeks in a month.

moon
der Mond

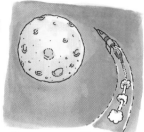

Die
Astronauten flogen zum Mond.
The astronauts went to the moon.

more*
mehr

Jimmy
möchte
mehr Milch.
Jimmy wants more milk.

morning
der Morgen

Wir essen
jeden Morgen Frühstück.
We have breakfast every morning.

mosquito
die Mücke

Eine Mücke stach mich!
A mosquito bit me!

moth
die Motte

Die Motte
sieht wie ein Schmetterling aus.
The moth looks like a butterfly.

mother
die Mutter

Meine Mutter liest mir vor.
My mother reads to me.

mountain
der Berg

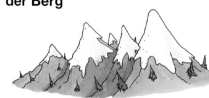

Die
Berge sind
mit Schnee bedeckt.
The mountains are covered with snow.

mouse*
die Maus

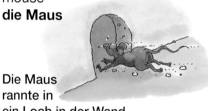

Die Maus
rannte in
ein Loch in der Wand.
The mouse ran
into a hole in the wall.

mouth
der Mund

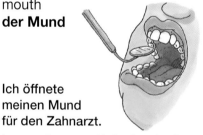

Ich öffnete
meinen Mund
für den Zahnarzt.
I opened my mouth for the dentist.

movie
der Film

Die
Kinder sahen sich einen Film an.
The children watched a movie.

much
viel

Es gibt hier zu viel zu essen!
There is too much to eat here!

mud
**der
Schlamm**
Schweine
wälzen sich
gern im Schlamm.

Pigs love to roll around in the mud.

museum
das Museum

Ein Museum hat viele Statuen.
A museum contains many statues.

mushroom
der Pilz

Wir fanden
Pilze im
nassen
Gras.
We found
mushrooms in the wet grass.

music
die Musik

Helene schrieb
neue Musik
für die Kapelle.
Helen wrote
new music for the band.

mustache
der Schnurrbart

Roberts
Onkel hat
einen langen
Schnurrbart.
Robert's uncle
has a long mustache.

mustard
der Senf

Senf ist
gut auf
Schinkenbroten.
Mustard is good
on ham sandwiches.

NnNnNnNn

nail
nageln

Robert nagelte das Schild an den Zaun.

Robert nailed the sign to the fence.

nail
der Nagel

Robert benutzte vier Nägel.

Robert used four nails.

name
der Name

Wessen Name ist *Jimmy*?

Whose name is *Jimmy*?

nap
das Nickerchen

Großpapa macht ein Nickerchen.

Grandpa is taking a nap.

nap
schlummern

Er schlummert auf dem Sofa.

He is napping on the sofa.

napkin
die Serviette

Maria ließ ihre Serviette fallen.

Mary dropped her napkin.

narrow
schmal

Der Briefkasten ist zu schmal.

The mailbox is too narrow.

near
nahe

Die Lampe ist nahe dem Stuhl.

The lamp is near the chair.

neck
der Hals

Giraffen haben lange Hälse.

Giraffes have long necks.

necklace
die Kette

Helene trägt eine goldene Kette.

Helen is wearing a gold necklace.

necktie
die Krawatte

Robert trägt eine Krawatte.

Robert is wearing a necktie.

need
brauchen

Wir brauchen mehr Milch.

We need more milk.

needle
die Nadel

Großmama näht mit einer Nadel.

Grandma sews with a needle.

nest
das Nest

Die kleinen Vögel warten im Nest.

The baby birds are waiting in the nest.

net
das Netz

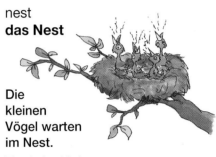

Ich schlug den Volleyball über das Netz.

I hit the volleyball over the net.

never
niemals

Die Lehrerin kommt niemals zu spät!

The teacher is never late!

new
neu

Stephan braucht neue Schuhe.

Steven needs new shoes.

newspaper
die Zeitung

Helene liest
die Zeitung.

Helen is reading
the newspaper.

---

night
die Nacht

Die Nächte
in den Bergen sind ruhig.

Nights are quiet in the mountains.

---

noise
der Lärm

Der Papagei macht zuviel Lärm.

The parrot makes too much noise.

---

noodles
die Nudeln

Meine Tante
kochte Nudeln zum Mittagessen.

My aunt cooked noodles for lunch.

---

noon
der Mittag

Wilhelm ist
bis Mittag
hungrig.

William is
hungry by noon.

---

nose
die Nase

Im Winter
wird meine
Nase rot.

In the winter my
nose becomes red.

---

note
die Notiz
Wilhelm wird
eine Notiz
von der
Adresse machen.

William will make
a note of the address.

---

notebook
das Taschenbuch

Er schreibt die
Adresse in sein
Taschenbuch.

He is writing the
address in his notebook.

---

notepad
**der
Notizblock**

Neben dem Telefon
ist ein Notizblock.

There is a notepad
near the telephone.

---

number
die Nummer

In meiner
Adresse
sind Nummern.

There are numbers in my address.

---

nurse
**die Kranken-
schwester**

Eine Krankenschwester
hilft Patienten gesund zu werden.

A nurse helps make patients healthy.

---

nut
die Nuß

Marias
Eiscreme ist mit
Nüssen bedeckt.

Mary's ice cream
has nuts on top.

OoOoOoOo

Oo

oar
das Ruder

Die Ruder sind im Ruderboot.

The oars are in the rowboat.

---

ocean
der Ozean

Walfische
leben im Ozean.

Whales live in the ocean.

---

octopus
der Krake

Ein Krake hat acht Arme.

An octopus has eight arms.

---

off
herab

Stephan fiel
von seinem Pferd herab.

Steven fell off his horse.

---

office
das Büro

Mein Papa
geht ins Büro zur Arbeit.

My dad goes to an office to work.

48

often
oft

Das Licht der
Verkehrsampel
wechselt oft.

The traffic light changes often.

---

oil
das Öl

Autos müssen Öl
und Benzin haben.

Cars have to have oil and gasoline.

---

old
alt

Maria trug ein
neues Hemd
und ihre
alten Jeans.

Mary wore a
new shirt and
her old jeans.

---

omelet
das Omelett

Ich kochte
ein Omelett
mit Eiern
und Käse.

I cooked an omelet
with eggs and cheese.

---

on
auf

Robert ist auf dem Fahrrad.

Robert is on the bicycle.

---

onion
die Zwiebel

Mein Papa ißt
Zwiebeln auf
seinem Hamburger.

My dad eats onions
on his hamburger.

---

open
öffnen

Das Baby öffnete
seinen Mund um zu weinen.

The baby opened her mouth to cry.

---

open
offen

Der Regen
kam durch das
offene Fenster.

The rain came
in the open window.

---

orange
orange

Mische rot
und gelb
um orange
zu machen.

Mix red and yellow to make orange.

---

orange
die Apfelsine

Robert aß eine
Apfelsine zum Mittagessen.

Robert ate an orange for lunch.

---

orchestra
das Orchester

Das Orchester
spielte länger
als eine
Stunde!

The orchestra
played for more
than an hour!

---

ostrich
der Strauß

Der Strauß
ist ein sehr
großer Vogel.

The ostrich is
a very large bird.

---

other
ander

Das andere Stück
Kuchen gehört dir!

The other piece of cake is yours!

---

out
aus

Stephan
ging aus der Tür.

Steven went out the door.

---

outside
die Außenseite

Die Außenseite
des Kastens ist gold.

The outside of the box is gold.

---

oven
der Ofen

Der Koch
backte eine Torte im Ofen.

The cook baked a pie in the oven.

---

over
über

Das Flugzeug
flog über unser Haus.

The airplane flew over our house.

---

owl
die Eule

Eulen sind
nachts auf
Nahrungssuche.

Owls hunt for food at night.

Pp*Pp*Pp*Pp*

package
das Paket

Im Briefkasten
war ein
Paket für mich.

There was a package
for me in the mailbox.

page
die Seite

Jimmy
zeichnete
auf dieser Seite.

Jimmy drew on this page.

pail
der Eimer

Jimmy nahm
seinen Eimer
zum Strand.

Jimmy took his pail to the beach.

pain
der Schmerz
Robert hatte
einen Schmerz
in seinem Kopf.

Robert had a pain in his head.

paint
malen

Helene malte ein Bild
von ihrer Katze.

Helen painted
a picture
of her cat.

paint
die Farbe
Die rote
Farbe tropfte auf den Teppich.

The red paint dripped on the rug.

paintbrush
der Malpinsel

Stephan
steckte den
Malpinsel
in die Farbe.

Steven put the
paintbrush into the paint.

pajamas
die Pyjamas

Maria trägt
Pyjamas
mit Füßen.

Mary wears pajamas with feet.

palace
der Palast

Der König und die
Königin wohnen in einem Palast.

The king and queen live in a palace.

pan
die Pfanne

Mutter
kocht Eier in einer Pfanne.

Mother cooks eggs in a pan.

panda
der Panda

Der Zoo
hat einen neuen Panda.

The zoo has a new panda.

pants
die Hosen

Robert
trug ein
weißes
Hemd und
schwarze Hosen.

Robert wore a
white shirt and
black pants.

paper
das Papier

Helenes
Papier ist
an dem
Anschlagbrett.

Helen's paper
is on the bulletin board.

parachute
der Fallschirm

Der Mann sprang
mit einem Fallschirm
aus dem Flugzeug.

The man jumped
from the airplane
with a parachute.

parade
die Parade

Clowns waren in der Parade.

There were clowns in the parade.

paramedic
der Sanitäter

Sanitäter
helfen
Leuten die
verletzt sind.

Paramedics
help people
who are hurt.

parents
die Eltern

Meine
Eltern sind Mama und Papa.

My parents are Mommy and Daddy.

park
der Park

Unser
Park
hat Gras,
Blumen, und Bänke.

Our park has grass,
flowers, and benches.

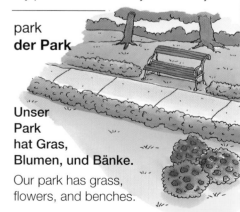

parrot
der Papagei

Tante
Alices
Papagei
spricht zu ihr.

Aunt Alice's parrot talks to her.

---

part
der Teil

Der Junge
aß einen
Teil des Apfels.

The boy ate part of the apple.

---

party
die Feier

Jimmy hat
eine Geburtstagsfeier.

Jimmy is having a birthday party.

---

passenger
der Passagier

Passagiere
kaufen
Fahrkarten
um mit dem
Zug zu fahren.

Passengers buy
tickets to ride the train.

---

paste
der Klebstoff

Jemand ließ den Klebstoff
auf dem Tisch.

Someone left
the paste on
the table.

paste
kleben

Thomas
klebte sein
Bild auf
die Seite.

Thomas pasted
his picture on the page.

---

pasture
die Weide

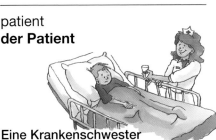

Die Kühe
sind auf der Weide.

The cows are in the pasture.

---

path
der Pfad

Wilhelm folgte
einem Pfad in dem Wald.

William followed a path in the forest.

---

patient
der Patient

Eine Krankenschwester
gibt dem Patienten Medizin.

A nurse gives the patient medicine.

---

paw
die Pfote

Der Hund hielt
seine Pfote hoch.

The dog held up its paw.

---

pea
die Erbse

Ich mag
Erbsen und Möhren.

I like peas and carrots.

---

peach
der Pfirsich

Robert aß
einen Pfirsich mit seinem Müsli.

Robert ate a peach with his cereal.

---

peanut
die Erdnuß

Helene
ißt Erdnüsse
im Kino.

Helen eats peanuts at the movies.

---

pear
die Birne

Hier
sind zwei Birnen und ein Apfel.

Here are two pears and an apple.

---

pebble
der Stein

Susanne
warf einen
Stein ins
Wasser.

Susan threw a
pebble into the water.

---

pen
der Füllhalter

Der Student
schrieb mit einem Füllhalter.

The student wrote with a pen.

---

pencil
der Bleistift

Wilhelm
zeichnet Bilder mit einem Bleistift.

William draws pictures with a pencil.

---

pencil sharpener
der Bleistiftspitzer

Im
Klassen-
zimmer
gibt es einen
Bleistiftspitzer.

There is a pencil
sharpener in the classroom.

penguin
der Pinguin

Pinguine
leben auf dem Eis.

Penguins live on the ice.

people
die Leute

Zwei Leute
kamen zu unserem Haus.

Two people came to our house.

pepper
der Pfeffer

Pfeffer ist
schwarz und
Salz ist weiß.

Pepper is black, and salt is white.

person
die Person

Eine Person
kam spät zur Schule.

One person was late for school.

pet
das Haustier

Das
Hündchen
ist Susannes
Haustier.

The puppy
is Susan's pet.

pet
streicheln

Susanne
streichelt ihr Hündchen.

Susan is petting her puppy.

petal
das Blütenblatt

Diese Blume
hat weiche,
rote Blütenblätter.

This flower has
soft, red petals.

pharmacist
der Apotheker
die Apothekerin

Tante Alice
kauft Pillen
beim Apotheker.

Aunt Alice buys pills
from the pharmacist.

pharmacy
die Apotheke

In der Apotheke
wird Medizin verkauft.

The pharmacy sells medicine.

phone booth
die Telefonzelle

Papa ruft
von einer
Telefonzelle
zu Hause an.

Dad is calling
home from a
phone booth.

photograph
das Foto

Maria trägt
ein Foto von
ihrem Papa.

Mary is carrying
a photograph of her dad.

piano
**das
Piano**

Robert
spielt das
Piano während
seine Schwester singt.

Robert plays the piano
while his sister sings.

picnic
das Picknick

Wir
aßen Huhn
auf unserem Picknick.

We ate chicken at our picnic.

picture
das Bild

In einem
Museum
hängen Bilder
an der Wand.

In a museum,
pictures hang on the walls.

pie
die Torte

Wer aß ein
Stück Torte?

Who ate a piece of pie?

piece
das Stück

Das ist
ein sehr großes Stück!

This is a very large piece!

pig
das Schwein

Es gibt viele
Schweine auf
Onkel Eduards Farm.

There are many pigs
on Uncle Edward's farm.

piggy bank
das Sparschwein

Maria bewahrt
Geld in ihrem
Sparschwein auf.

Mary keeps money
in her piggy bank.

pile
der Haufen

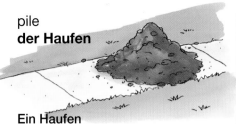

Ein Haufen
Dreck bedeckte den Fußweg.

A pile of dirt covered the sidewalk.

---

pill
die Pille

Die Krankenschwester
gab Thomas eine gelbe Pille.

The nurse gave Thomas a yellow pill.

---

pillow
das Kissen

Mein Bett hat
weiche Kissen für meinen Kopf.

My bed has soft pillows for my head.

---

pilot
der Pilot

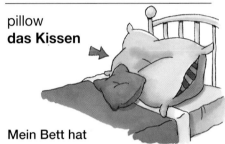

Der Pilot fliegt das Flugzeug.

The pilot is flying the airplane.

---

pin
die Nadel

Nadeln
sind sehr scharf!

Pins are very sharp!

---

pineapple
die Ananas

Susanne
tat Ananas
in den
Obstsalat.

Susan put
pineapple
in the fruit salad.

---

pink
rosa

Susanne
trug
einen
rosa Hut
und Mantel.

Susan wore a pink hat and coat.

---

pitcher
der Ballwerfer
die Ballwerferin

Maria ist die
Ballwerferin ihrer
Baseballmannschaft.

Mary is the pitcher
on her baseball team.

---

pitcher
der Krug

Thomas
verschüttete
Milch aus
dem Krug.

Thomas spilled
the milk pitcher.

---

place
der Platz

Ein Bett ist
ein Platz zum Schlafen.

A bed is a place for sleeping.

---

plain
einfach

Das
Geschenk
kam in
einfachem
Papier ohne Bänder.

The gift came in
plain paper with no ribbons.

---

plain
das Flachland

Weizen
wächst auf dem Flachland.

Wheat grows on the plains.

---

planet
der Planet

Die Planeten
umkreisen die Sonne.

The planets circle the sun.

---

plant
pflanzen

Der Farmer
pflanzt Mais.

The farmer is planting corn.

---

plant
die Pflanze

Das Fenster
ist voller Pflanzen.

The window is full of plants.

---

plate
der Teller

Wilhelm hat
Fleisch und
Kartoffeln
auf seinem
Teller.

William has meat
and potatoes on his plate.

---

play
spielen

Maria
spielt Gitarre.

Mary plays the guitar.

---

play
spielen

Die Kinder
spielen auf
den Schaukeln.

The children are
playing on the swings.

playground
der Spielplatz

Robert geht
nach der Schule
auf den Spielplatz.
Robert goes to the
playground after school.

please
bitte

Mehr
Kuchen,
bitte.
More cake, please.

plumber
der Klempner

Ein Klempner kam um
das Waschbecken zu reparieren.
A plumber came to fix the sink.

pocket
die Tasche

Was ist
in deiner Tasche?
What is in your pocket?

point
zeigen

Susanne
zeigt auf die Katze.
Susan is pointing at the cat.

point
die Spitze

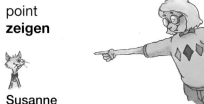

Die Nadel
hat eine scharfe Spitze.
The needle has a sharp point.

polar bear
der Eisbär

Eisbären
haben ein weißes Fell.
Polar bears have white fur.

police
die Polizei

Die Polizei
beschützt uns.
The police keep us safe.

police car
das Polizeiauto

Ein Polizeiauto
raste die Straße hinab.
A police car raced down the street.

policeman*
der Polizist

Ein Polizist gab meinem
Papa einen Strafzettel.
A policeman gave my dad a ticket.

policewoman*
die Polizistin

Die
Polizistin
zeigte
mir den Weg.
The policewoman
showed me the way.

pond
der Teich

Frösche
und Fische leben im Teich.
Frogs and fish live in the pond.

ponytail
der Pferdeschwanz

Maria band
eine Schleife
um ihren
Pferdeschwanz.
Mary tied a ribbon
around her ponytail.

pool
das Schwimmbecken

Wir schwimmen und spielen
in einem Schwimmbecken.
We swim and play in a pool.

popcorn
das Popcorn

Stephan
kauft Popcorn
im Kino.
Steven buys popcorn at the movies.

porch
die Veranda

Ich
sitze beim Sonnenuntergang
gern auf der Veranda.
I love to sit on the porch at sunset.

porthole
das Bullauge

Ein Bullauge
ist ein Fenster auf einem Schiff.
A porthole is a window on a boat.

post office
das Postamt

Helene kauft
Briefmarken
auf dem Postamt.
Helen buys stamps
at the post office.

pot
der Topf

Susanne rührt im Suppentopf.
Susan is stirring the pot of soup.

potato
die Kartoffel

Großmama schnitt Kartoffeln um Pommes Frites zu machen.
Grandma cut up potatoes to make french fries.

potato chips
die Kartoffelchips

Robert aß Kartoffelchips auf dem Picknick.
Robert ate potato chips at the picnic.

powder
pudern

Maria puderte das Baby.
Mary powdered the baby.

practice
üben

Helene übt auf der Geige.
Helen is practicing the violin.

present
das Geschenk

Diese Geburtstagsgeschenke sind für Jimmy.
These birthday presents are for Jimmy.

pretty
schön

Der Garten ist voll mit schönen Blumen.
The garden is filled with pretty flowers.

price
der Preis

Die Preise für das Essen stehen auf der Speisekarte.
The prices for the food are on the menu.

prince
der Prinz

Ein Prinz ist der Sohn eines Königs und einer Königin.
A prince is the son of a king and queen.

princess
die Prinzessin

Die Prinzessin trug eine kleine Krone.
The princess wore a small crown.

prize
der Preis

Robert gewann einen Preis für sein schnelles Laufen.
Robert won a prize for running fast.

puddle
die Pfütze

Die Kinder gingen durch die Pfützen.
The children walked through the puddles.

pull
ziehen

Maria zog den Wagen den Fußweg entlang.
Mary pulled the wagon down the sidewalk.

pumpkin
der Kürbis

Mama schnitzte ein Gesicht in meinen Kürbis.
Mommy carved a face in my pumpkin.

puppet
die Puppe

Wilhelm hat eine Puppe auf seiner Hand.
William has a puppet on his hand.

puppy
das Hündchen

Ich liebe mein neues Hündchen!
I love my new puppy!

purple
purpur

Der Traubensaft ist purpur.
The grape juice is purple.

purse
die Tasche

Susanne trägt ihre Tasche über ihrer Schulter.
Susan carries her purse on her shoulder.

push
schieben

Stephan
schob seinen Teller weg.

Steven pushed his plate away.

put*
legen

Stephan
legte seine Hand auf seinen Kopf.

Steven put his hand on his head.

puzzle
das Rätsel

Dieses Rätsel
ist zu schwer.

This puzzle is too hard.

QqQqQqQq

queen
die Königin

Die Königin
trägt
Juwelen
und eine Krone.

The queen wears
jewels and a crown.

quiet
ruhig

SSSSHHHH

Bitte sei ruhig.

Please be quiet.

RrRrRrRr

rabbit
das Kaninchen

Thomas
Haustier ist ein
weißes Kaninchen.

Thomas's pet is a white rabbit.

race
rennen

Ich renne mit dir bis zum
Baum um die Wette.

I will race you
to the tree.

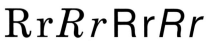

race
der Wettlauf

Wer wird in
diesem Wettlauf siegen?

Who will win this race?

radio
das Radio

Helenes
Radio ist zu laut.

Helen's radio is too loud.

rag
der Lappen

Thomas putzte
den Schmutz
mit einem
Lappen weg.

Thomas cleaned up
the mess with a rag.

rain
der Regen

Von den
dunkelen
Wolken
kam Regen.

Rain came from
the dark clouds.

rainbow
der Regenbogen

Am Himmel
war ein Regenbogen.

There was a rainbow in the sky.

raincoat
der Regenmantel

Susanne hat
einen gelben
Regenmantel.

Susan has
a yellow raincoat.

rake
die Harke

Wilhelm
harkt die
Blätter mit einer Harke.

William rakes the leaves with a rake.

ranch
die Ranch

Cowboys
leben auf Ranches.

Cowboys live on ranches.

raspberries
die Himbeeren

Maria aß
Himbeeren zu
ihrer Eiscreme.

Mary ate raspberries
with her ice cream.

rat
die Ratte

Die Katze
lief der Ratte nach.

The cat ran after the rat.

---

read*
lesen

Wilhelm liest Jimmy
eine Geschichte vor.

William is reading Jimmy a story.

---

receive
bekommen

Maria bekam
ein Geschenk von Wilhelm.

Mary received a gift from William.

---

red
rot

Äpfel,
Kirschen, und
Himbeeren
sind rot.

Apples, cherries,
and raspberries are red.

---

refrigerator
**der
Kühlschrank**

Milch wird
im Kühlschrank
aufbewahrt.

Milk is kept in the refrigerator.

---

reins
die Zügel

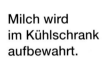

Wilhelm
lenkt sein Pferd
durch das
Ziehen an den Zügeln.

William steers his
horse by pulling the reins.

---

relative
der Verwandte
die Verwandte

Meine Tante
und Onkel sind
zwei meiner
Verwandten.

My aunt and uncle
are two of my relatives.

---

reporter
der Reporter

Jener Reporter
schreibt für eine Zeitung.

That reporter writes for a newspaper.

---

reptile
das Reptil

Schlangen
und Alligatoren sind Reptilien.

Snakes and alligators are reptiles.

---

restaurant
das Restaurant

Stephan
und sein
Papa hatten
Abendessen
in einem Restaurant.

Steven and his dad
ate dinner at a restaurant.

---

rhinoceros
das Nashorn

Das Nashorn
ist ein großes
Tier mit
einem Horn.

The rhinoceros
is a large animal
with a horn.

---

ribbon
die Schleife

Susannes
Mutter band
eine Schleife
in ihr Haar.

Susan's mother
tied a ribbon in her hair.

---

rice
der Reis

Helene
mag Huhn mit Reis.

Helen likes chicken with rice.

---

ride*
fahren

Wilhelm fährt
mit seinem Fahrrad zur Schule.

William rides his bicycle to school.

---

right
recht

Maria legte
ihre rechte Hand
auf ihr Herz.

Mary put her right
hand on her heart.

---

right
richtig

Welcher
ist der
richtige Weg?

Which is the right way?

---

ring*
läuten

Wilhelm
läutet die
Dinnerglocke.

William is ringing the dinner bell.

---

ring
der Ring

Mama
trägt einen Ehering.

Mom wears a wedding ring.

river
der Fluß

Siehst du
den Fluß im Tal?

Do you see the river in the valley?

road
die Straße

Jene Straße
führt in den Wald.

That road goes into the forest.

roar
brüllen

Der Löwe
brüllte um Nahrung.

The lion roared for food.

roast
braten

Helene briet einen Truthahn
im Ofen.

Helen roasted
a turkey in
the oven.

roast
der Braten

Der Braten
kochte stundenlang!

The roast cooked for hours!

robe
der Morgenmantel

Robert
trägt einen
Morgenmantel
über seinem
Pyjama.

Robert wears
a robe over
his pajamas.

robin
das Rotkehlchen

Die Eier des
Rotkehlchens sind blau.

Robins' eggs are blue.

rock
der Stein

Maria
fand einen
schönen
Stein am
Strand.

Mary found
a pretty rock on the beach.

rock
schaukeln

Onkel
Eduard
sitzt und
schaukelt gern.

Uncle Edward loves to sit and rock.

roll
rollen

Mein
Hund
kann sich
überrollen und hübsch machen.

My dog can roll over and sit up.

roller skates
die Rollschuhe

Helene läuft
schnell auf ihren
Rollschuhen.

Helen goes fast
on her roller skates.

roof
das Dach

Unser Haus
hat ein rotes Dach.

Our house has a red roof.

room
das Zimmer

Stephan hat sein eigenes Zimmer.

Steven has his own room.

rooster
der Hahn

Der Hahn steht auf dem Zaun.

The rooster is standing on the fence.

rope
das Seil

Wilhelm
band ein Seil
an seinen Wagen.

William tied a rope to his wagon.

rose
die Rose

Rosen
riechen so gut!

Roses smell so good!

round
rund

Der Ball
ist rund.

The ball is round.

rowboat
das Ruderboot

Der
Fischer sitzt in
einem Ruderboot auf dem See.

The fisherman sits in a
rowboat on the lake.

rub
reiben

Thomas reibt sein Gesicht mit einem Handtuch.

Thomas rubs his face with a towel.

rug
der Teppich

Die Katze schlummert auf dem Teppich.

The cat is napping on the rug.

ruler
das Lineal

Thomas zieht die Linie mit einem Lineal.

Thomas draws the line with a ruler.

run*
laufen

Helene läuft schneller als Susanne.

Helen runs faster than Susan.

runner
der Läufer
die Läuferin

Die Läufer laufen sehr schnell.

The runners are going very fast.

Ss Ss Ss Ss

sack
der Sack

Stephan trägt sein Mittagessen in einem Sack.

Steven carries his lunch in a sack.

sad
traurig

Der kleine Junge ist traurig.

The little boy is sad.

saddle
der Sattel

Helene saß im Sattel auf dem Pferd.

Helen sat in the saddle on the horse.

safe
sicher

Sitzgurte halten uns im Auto sicher.

Seat belts keep us safe in the car.

safe
der Tresor

Onkel Eduard bewahrt sein Geld in einem Tresor auf.

Uncle Edward keeps his money in a safe.

sail
segeln

Ein kleines Boot segelte auf dem See.

A small boat sailed on the lake.

sailboat
das Segelboot

Ein Segelboot ist am Anleger festgemacht.

A sailboat is tied to the dock.

sailor
der Matrose

Matrosen tragen saubere Uniformen.

Sailors wear clean uniforms.

salad
der Salat

Stephan aß einen Salat zu seinem Abendessen.

Steven ate a salad with his dinner.

salt
der Salz

Wilhelm streute Salz auf das Popcorn.

William added salt to the popcorn.

sand
der Sand

Wir bauten ein Schloß aus Sand.

We built a castle from sand.

sandals
die Sandalen

Susanne
trägt
Sandalen
im Sommer.
Susan wears
sandals in
the summer.

sandbox
die Sandkiste

Wilhelm spielt in der Sandkiste.
William is playing in the sandbox.

sandwich
das Butterbrot

Roberts
Butterbrot
ist mit Schinken
und Käse belegt.
Robert's sandwich
has ham and cheese on it.

Santa Claus
**der
Weihnachtsmann**

Hat der
Weihnachtsmann ein
Geschenk für dich?
Does Santa Claus
have a present for you?

saucer
die Untertasse

Etwas Tee
lief auf die
Untertasse.
Some tea spilled into the saucer.

sausage
die Wurst

Maria aß
Wurst und
Eier zum
Frühstück.
Mary ate sausage
and eggs for breakfast.

saw
sägen

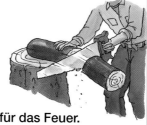

Papa sägte
Holzscheite für das Feuer.
Dad sawed logs for the fire.

saxophone
das Saxophon

Maria
lernt Saxophon
spielen.
Mary is learning
to play the saxophone.

scale
die Schuppe

Mein Fisch
ist mit goldenen
Schuppen bedeckt.
My pet fish is
covered with gold scales.

scale
die Waage

Der schwere
Mann stand
auf der Waage.
The heavy man
stood on the scale.

scarecrow
die Vogelscheuche

Die Vogelscheuche
hält die Vögel fern.
The scarecrow keeps the birds away.

scarf*
der Schal

Maria
trug einen
rosa Schal
um ihren Hals.
Mary wore a pink
scarf around her neck.

school
die Schule

Die Schule ist ein
rotes Backsteingebäude.
The school is a red-brick building.

school bus
der Schulbus

Der
Schulbus ist groß und gelb.
The school bus is big and yellow.

scientist
**der Wissenschaftler
die Wissenschaftlerin**

Der
Wissen-
schaftler
benutzt sein
Mikroskop.
The scientist is
using his microscope.

scissors
die Schere

Susanne
schnitt
Papierpuppen
mit der
Schere aus.
Susan cut paper
dolls with the scissors.

screw
die Schraube
Schrauben halten Dinge
zusammen.
Screws hold things
together.

screwdriver
der Schraubenzieher
Papa benutzt den
Schraubenzieher.
Dad is using the screwdriver.

sea
das Meer

Wale und
Haifische schwimmen im Meer.
Whales and sharks swim in the sea.

seal
der Seehund
Der Seehund
kann einen
Korbball auf
seiner Nase
fangen.
The seal can
catch a basketball on its nose.

seashell
die Muschel

Thomas
fand einige
Muscheln
am Strand.
Thomas found
some seashells at the beach.

seat
der Sitz

Thomas saß
in einem Sitz in der Nähe der Tür.
Thomas sat in a seat near the door.

seat belt
der Sitzgurt

Schnalle deinen
Sitzgurt im Flugzeug an.
Wear your seat belt in the airplane.

seaweed
der Seetang

Der Seetang
wächst im Ozean.
Seaweed grows in the ocean.

secretary
**der Sekretär
die Sekretärin**

Die Sekretärin
hat einen
Computer auf ihrem Schreibtisch.
The secretary has a
computer at her desk.

see*
sehen

Ich
kann den Zug kommen sehen.
I can see the train coming.

seed
die Saat

Der Vogel ißt Saaten.
The bird is eating seeds.

seesaw
die Wippe

Der Wippe geht auf und ab.
The seesaw goes up and down.

sell*
verkaufen

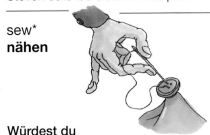

Stephan
verkauft Eiscreme im Park.
Steven sells ice cream in the park.

sew*
nähen

Würdest du
diesen Knopf annähen?
Could you sew this button on?

sewing machine
die Nähmaschine

Mama macht
Kleider auf
der Nähmaschine.
Mom makes clothes
on the sewing machine.

shadow
der Schatten

Die Katze
spielt mit ihrem Schatten.
The cat is playing with its shadow.

shark
der Haifisch

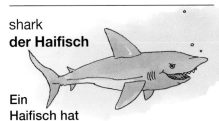

Ein
Haifisch hat
eine Flosse auf seinem Rücken.
A shark has a fin on its back.

sharp
scharf

Stephan zerschnitt die Schnur
mit einem scharfen Messer.
Steven cut the string
with a sharp knife.

sheep*
das Schaf

Das Schaf lief vor dem Hunde weg.
The sheep ran away from the dog.

sheet
das Bettuch

Auf Helenes
Bett sind saubere Bettücher.
Helen's bed has clean sheets on it.

shelf*
das Regal
Das Müsli ist auf dem unteren Regal.
The cereal is on the bottom shelf.

ship
das Schiff
Dieses große Schiff segelt auf dem Ozean.
This big ship sails on the ocean.

shipwreck
das Schiffs-wrack
Am Ufer ist ein altes Schiffswrack.
There is an old shipwreck on the shore.

shirt
das Hemd
Maria trägt das Baseballhemd ihrer Mannschaft.
Mary wears her team's baseball shirt.

shoe
der Schuh
Wessen rote Schuhe sind dies?
Whose red shoes are these?

shoelace
das Schnürband
Thomas Schuhe haben schwarze Schnürbänder.
Thomas's shoes have black shoelaces.

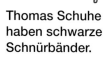

shop
der Laden
Wilhelm ist in einem Spielzeugladen.
William is in a toy shop.

shop
einkaufen
Er kauft ein, um ein Geschenk zu kaufen.
He is shopping for a gift.

shore
das Ufer
Wir saßen am Ufer und beobachteten die Boote.
We sat on the shore and watched the boats.

short
klein
Stephan ist klein, aber Susanne ist groß.
Steven is short, but Susan is tall.

shorts
die Shorts
Helene trägt Shorts um Ball zu spielen.
Helen wears shorts to play ball.

shoulder
die Schulter
Der Papagei saß auf Susannes Schulter.
The parrot sat on Susan's shoulder.

shovel
die Schaufel
Der Bauer gräbt mit einer Schaufel.
The farmer is digging with a shovel.

show*
zeigen
Stephan zeigt uns seine Uhr.
Steven is showing us his watch.

show*
sich zeigen
Die Sonne zeigt sich ein wenig.
The sun is showing a little bit.

shower
die Dusche
Thomas ist in der Dusche.
Thomas is in the shower.

sick
krank
Wilhelm ist sehr krank.
William is very sick.

side
die Seite
Thomas hat einen Schmerz in der Seite.
Thomas has a pain in his side.

62

sidewalk
der Bürgersteig

Das Mädchen spielt mit einem Sprungseil auf dem Bürgersteig.

The girl jumps rope on the sidewalk.

---

sign
das Schild

Im Hof dieses Hauses ist ein Schild.

There is a sign in the yard of this house.

---

signature
die Unterschrift

Maria schrieb ihre Unterschrift auf das Papier.

Mary wrote her signature on the paper.

---

silly
komisch

Wir lachen, wenn Großpapa einen komischen Hut trägt.

We laugh when Grandpa wears a silly hat.

---

silver
silbern

Wilhelm hat einen silbernen Ring.

William has a silver ring.

---

sing*
singen

Maria singt für ihre Klasse.

Mary is singing for her class.

singer
der Sänger
die Sängerin

Sie ist eine sehr laute Sängerin.

She is a very loud singer.

---

sink
das Spülbecken

Helene wusch das Geschirr in dem Spülbecken.

Helen washed the dishes in the sink.

---

sister
die Schwester

Ich halte meine kleine Schwester auf meinem Schoß.

I hold my little sister on my lap.

---

sit*
sitzen

Jimmy sitzt aufrecht auf dem Stuhl.

Jimmy sits up straight in the chair.

---

size
die Größe

Hat dieses Hemd die richtige Größe?

Is this shirt the right size?

---

skate
der Schlittschuh

Thomas hat neue Schlittschuhe.

Thomas has some new skates.

---

skate
Schlittschuh laufen

Er läuft Schlittschuh auf dem Teich.

He is skating on the pond.

---

skateboard
das Rollschuhbrett

Wilhelm fährt mit seinem Rollschuhbrett.

William is riding his skateboard.

---

ski
der Ski

Mama legte unsere Skier auf das Wagendach.

Mom put our skis on the car top.

---

ski
skilaufen

Wir alle gehen skilaufen.

We are all going skiing.

---

skirt
der Rock

Auf meinem Rock sind Blumen.

My skirt has flowers on it.

---

skunk
das Stinktier

Das Stinktier hat einen furchtbaren Geruch.

The skunk has a terrible smell.

---

sky
der Himmel

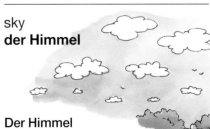

Der Himmel ist voll weißer Wolken.

The sky is full of white clouds.

skyscraper
der Wolkenkratzer

Ein Wolkenkratzer
ist ein
sehr hohes
Gebäude.

A skyscraper
is a very
tall building.

sled
der Schlitten

Maria
fährt mit
ihrem Schlitten
den Hügel hinunter.

Mary is riding her
sled down the hill.

sleep*
schlafen

Schhh, das Baby schläft.
Shhh, the baby is sleeping.

sleeve
der Ärmel

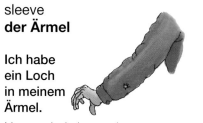

Ich habe
ein Loch
in meinem
Ärmel.

I have a hole in my sleeve.

slide*
rutschen

Die Kinder
rutschen auf dem Eis.
The children are sliding on the ice.

slow
langsam

Schildkröten sind langsam,
und Hasen sind schnell.
Turtles are slow, and rabbits are fast.

---

small
klein

Helene hat
ein kleines
Hündchen in
ihrem Haus.

Helen has a small
puppy at her house.

smell
der Geruch
Was für ein
guter Geruch
ist das?
What is that
good smell?

smell
riechen
Du riechst das Brot backen.
You smell the bread baking.

smile
lächeln
Maria lächelte
mich an.
Mary smiled at me.

smile
das Lächeln
Sie hat ein hübsches Lächeln.
She has a pretty smile.

smoke
der Rauch

Wo es Rauch gibt ist auch Feuer.
Where there is smoke, there is fire.

snack
der Imbiß

Thomas
nahm
einen Imbiß nach der Schule.
Thomas ate a snack after school.

---

snail
die Schnecke

Die Schnecke ist sehr langsam.
The snail is very slow.

snake
die Schlange

Schlangen sind
saubere, trockene Reptilien.
Snakes are clean, dry reptiles.

sneeze
niesen

Wenn
Maria Blumen
riecht niest sie.
When Mary smells
flowers she sneezes.

snow
der Schnee

Wilhelm
entfernt
den Schnee
vom
Fußweg.
William is
moving the snow off the sidewalk.

snowball
der Schneeball

Helene
bewarf ihren
Bruder mit
einem
Schneeball.
Helen threw a
snowball at her brother.

snowflake
die Schneeflocke

Während eines Schneesturmes
fallen viele Schneeflocken.
Many snowflakes fall in a snowstorm.

snowman*
der Schneemann

Die Kinder
bauten
einen
Schneemann
im Hof.

The children built
a snowman in the yard.

snowstorm
der Schneesturm

Letzte Nacht
gab es einen Schneesturm.

There was a snowstorm last night.

soap
die Seife

Maria reibt
sich Seife
auf ihre Hände.

Mary rubs the
soap on her hands.

socks
die Socken

Maria
trägt gelbe
Socken.

Mary is wearing
yellow socks.

sofa
das Sofa

Wir saßen
nahe dem
Kamin auf dem Sofa.

We sat on the sofa near the fireplace.

soft
weich

Das Fell
einer Katze ist weich.

A cat's fur is soft.

soft drink
die Limonade

Robert tat
Eis in seine
Limonade.

Robert put ice in his soft drink.

some
einige

Einige Blüten sind offen.
Some blossoms are open.

somersault
der Purzelbaum

Helene kann
einen Purzelbaum machen.
Helen can do a somersault.

son
der Sohn

Jene Frau
hat einen Sohn.
That woman has a son.

soon
bald

Ich
muß bald
zu Bett gehen.
I must go to bed soon.

soup
die Suppe

Stephan aß
Tomatensuppe
und Kräcker.
Steven ate tomato
soup and crackers.

space
der Platz

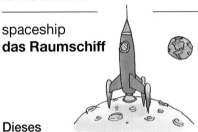

Da ist noch
Platz für
mehr Bücher.
There is space
for more books.

spaceship
das Raumschiff

Dieses
Raumschiff ist auf dem Mond.
This spaceship is on the moon.

sparrow
der Spatz

In dem
Baum sind
zwei Spatzen.
There are two
sparrows in the tree.

speak*
sprechen

Robert spricht zu Helene.
Robert is speaking to Helen.

spider
die Spinne

Eine große
schwarze Spinne
rannte die Wand hinauf.

A large, black spider ran up the wall.

spiderweb
das Spinngewebe

In der
Ecke
ist ein
Spinngewebe.

There is a spiderweb in the corner.

spill
vergießen

Wer vergoß die Milch?

Who spilled the milk?

spin*
drehen

Der Kreisel
dreht sich sehr schnell.

The top is spinning very fast.

spinach
der Spinat

Helene
pflanzte Spinat im Garten.

Helen planted spinach in the garden.

spoke
die Speiche

Einige Speichen sind gebrochen.

Some spokes are broken.

sponge
der Schwamm

Thomas
wischte den
nassen Tisch mit
einem Schwamm.

Thomas wiped the
wet table with a sponge.

spoon
der Löffel

Großvater
rührt seinen
Kaffee mit
einem Löffel um.

Grandfather stirs
his coffee with a spoon.

sports
der Sport

Robert
liebt Sport.

Robert loves sports.

spot
der Fleck

Mein Hund ist
weiß mit schwarzen Flecken.

My dog is white with black spots.

spotlight
der Scheinwerfer

Der Sänger
steht im Scheinwerferlicht.

The singer stands in the spotlight.

spread*
streichen

Maria strich
Butter auf
das heiße Brot.

Mary spread butter on the hot bread.

spring
der Frühling

Blumen
kommen im Frühling heraus.

Flowers come out in the spring.

sprinkler
der Sprenger

Ein Sprenger
wässert den Rasen.

A sprinkler waters the yard.

square
das Quadrat

Wie viele Quadrate sind da?

How many squares are there?

squeeze
drücken

Robert
drückte die
Ketchup-
flasche.

Robert squeezed the ketchup bottle.

squirrel
das Eichhörnchen

Ein
Eichhörnchen
lief den Baum
hinauf.

A squirrel
ran up the tree.

stable
der Stall

Die Pferde
schlafen im Stall.

The horses sleep in the stable.

stage
die Bühne

Die Kapelle sitzt auf der Bühne.

The band sits on the stage.

stairs
die Treppe

Helene ging
die Treppe
zu ihrem
Schlafzimmer
hinauf.

Helen walked up
the stairs to her bedroom.

---

stamp
stampfen

Maria war
verärgert
und stampfte
mit ihrem Fuß.

Mary was angry
and stamped her foot.

---

stamp
die Briefmarke

Die
Briefmarke
gehört auf den Umschlag.

The stamp goes on the envelope.

---

stand*
stehen

Bitte
stehe
gerade!

Please stand
up straight!

---

stapler
die Heftmaschine

Die Heftmaschine ist leer.

The stapler is empty.

---

staples
die Heftklammern

Maria tut Heftklammern
in die Heftmaschine.

Mary is putting staples in the stapler.

---

star
der Stern

Nachts sehen
wir die Sterne.

We see the stars at night.

---

starfish*
der Seestern

Helene fand
einen Seestern am Strand.

Helen found a starfish on the beach.

---

statue
die Statue

Die Statue
hat keinen
Kopf.

The statue
has no head.

---

steak
das Steak

Mein Papa
brät Steak
mit Pilzen.

My dad cooks
steak with mushrooms.

---

steer
steuern

Maria
steuerte
das Fahrrad
um das
Loch herum.

Mary steered the
bicycle around the hole.

---

stem
der Stengel

Die Blumen
haben sehr
lange
Stengel.

The flowers
have very
long stems.

---

step
die Stufe

Jimmy ging
zwei Stufen hoch.

Jimmy went up two steps.

---

stereo
das Stereo

Das Stereo
spielt schöne Musik.

The stereo is playing nice music.

---

stethoscope
**das
Stethoskop**

Der Doktor
hört mein
Herz mit einem
Stethoskop ab.

The doctor listens to
my heart with a stethoscope.

---

stick
der Stock

Helene
warf
ihrem Hund
einen Stock
zum Fangen zu.

Helen threw a stick
for her dog to catch.

---

stilts
die Stelzen

Der Mann
auf den
Stelzen
ist so hoch
wie das
Dach.

The man on stilts
is as tall as the roof.

---

stir
umrühren

Tante Alice
rührt die Soße um.

Aunt Alice is stirring the gravy.

stirrup
der Steigbügel

**Schieb deine Füße
in die Steigbügel.**
Slide your feet into the stirrups.

---

stone
der Stein

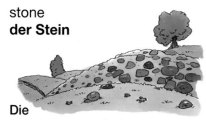

**Die
Mauer war aus Steinen gemacht.**
The wall was made of stones.

---

stop
halten

**Beim roten
Licht hielten wir das Auto an.**
We stopped the car for the red light.

---

stop sign
das Haltezeichen

**An der
Ecke ist ein
Haltezeichen.**
There is a stop
sign at the corner.

---

storm
der Sturm

**Regen,
Blitz, und Wind
kamen mit dem Sturm.**
Rain, lightning, and
wind came with the storm.

---

stove
der Herd

**Meine
Mama
kocht
heißen
Brei auf
dem Herd.**

My mom cooks hot
cereal on the stove.

---

straight (hair)
glatt

**Maria
hat
glattes Haar.**
Mary has
straight hair.

---

straw
der Strohhalm

**Stephan
trinkt Milch mit
einem Strohhalm.**
Steven drinks milk with a straw.

---

strawberry
die Erdbeere

**Wir aßen
Erdbeeren
zu unserer
Eiscreme.**
We ate strawberries
with our ice cream.

---

stream
der Strom

**Helene und
Susanne
sprangen über
den Strom.**
Helen and Susan
jumped over the stream.

---

street
die Straße

**Diese Straße ist für
Autos, nicht für Lastwagen.**
This street is for cars, not trucks.

---

string
die Schnur

**Robert band
die Pakete mit Schnur.**
Robert tied the packages with string.

---

stripe
der Streifen

**Jene Fahne
hat rote und
weiße Streifen.**
That flag has red
and white stripes on it.

---

stroller
der Kinderwagen

**Das Baby
ist im
Kinderwagen.**
The baby is
in the stroller.

---

strong
stark

Elefanten sind sehr stark.
Elephants are very strong.

---

student
der Schüler

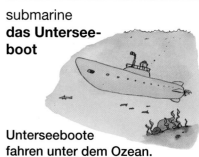

**Der
Schüler schreibt das Alphabet.**
The student is writing the alphabet.

---

submarine
**das Untersee-
boot**

**Unterseeboote
fahren unter dem Ozean.**
Submarines run under the ocean.

---

suds
die Seifenlauge

**Wasser und Seifenlauge
liefen auf den Boden.**
Water and suds spilled on the floor.

sugar
der Zucker

Susanne
tut Zucker
auf ihr Müsli.

Susan puts sugar on her cereal.

---

suit
der Anzug

Mein Anzug
hat eine
Hose und
eine Jacke.

My suit has pants and a jacket.

---

suitcase
der Koffer

Im Koffer
ist Platz
für mehr
Hemden.

There is space in the
suitcase for more shirts.

---

summer
der Sommer

Im Sommer ist das Wetter heiß.

The weather is hot in the summer.

---

sun
die Sonne

Die Sonne erleuchtet die Erde.

The sun lights up the Earth.

---

sunrise
der Sonnenaufgang

Bei
Sonnenaufgang
singen die Vögel.

The birds sing at sunrise.

---

sunset
der Sonnenuntergang

Sonnenuntergänge im
Winter können wunderbar sein.

Winter sunsets can be beautiful.

---

supermarket
der Supermarkt

Mama kauft
unser Essen
im Supermarkt.

Mom buys our food
at the supermarket.

---

surround
umgeben

Büsche umgeben den Hof.

Bushes surround the yard.

---

swan
der Schwan

Schwäne leben
in dem Teich im Park.

Swans live in the pond at the park.

---

sweater
der Pullover

Meine Großmutter
gab mir einen
neuen Pullover.

My grandmother
gave me a new sweater.

---

sweatpants
die Trainingshosen

Thomas
bekam
Trainingshosen
zu seinem
Geburtstag.

Thomas received
sweatpants for his birthday.

---

sweatshirt
das Trainingshemd

Maria zog ihr
Trainingshemd an.

Mary pulled on
her sweatshirt.

---

sweep*
kehren

Wilhelm
kehrt den Fußboden.

William is sweeping the floor.

---

swim*
schwimmen

Helene schwimmt
so schnell wie ein Fisch!

Helen swims as fast as a fish!

---

swing
die Schaukel

Robert hat eine
Schaukel in
seinem
Baum.

Robert has a swing
in his tree.

---

swing
schaukeln

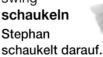

Stephan
schaukelt darauf.

Steven is swinging on it.

Tt *Tt* Tt *Tt*

table
der Tisch

Wir essen
Frühstück am
Küchentisch.

We eat breakfast
at the kitchen table.

tablecloth
die Tischdecke

Maria
legte eine
Tischdecke
auf den Tisch.

Mary spread a
tablecloth on the table.

tadpole
die Kaulquappe

Diese
Kaulquappe
wird zu einem
Frosch heranwachsen!

This tadpole will grow into a frog!

tail
der Schwanz

Der Löwe hat einen
sehr langen Schwanz.

The lion has a very long tail.

take*
nehmen

Helene nahm
zwei Stücke.

Helen took two pieces.

---

talk
sprechen

Thomas
spricht am Telefon.

Thomas is talking on the telephone.

tall
hoch

Ein Baum
ist sehr hoch.

One tree is very tall.

target
das Ziel

Helene traf
das Ziel mit ihrem Pfeil.

Helen hit the target with her arrow.

taxi
die Taxe

Robert
fuhr in einer Taxe zum Flugplatz.

Robert went to the airport in a taxi.

tea
der Tee

Meine
Mama trinkt
ihren Tee mit Zitrone.

My mom drinks her tea with lemon.

teach*
lehren

Susanne
lehrt Maria
Tennis zu spielen.

Susan is teaching
Mary to play tennis.

teacher
**der Lehrer
die Lehrerin**

Susanne
ist eine
gute Lehrerin.

Susan is a good teacher.

---

team
die Mannschaft

Es gibt
Mädchen
und Jungen
in meiner
Mannschaft.

There are girls and
boys on my team.

teeth*
die Zähne

Ich sehe
deine Zähne wenn du lächelst.

I see your teeth when you smile.

telephone
das Telefon

Maria hat ein
Telefon nahe ihrem Bett.

Mary has a telephone near her bed.

television
der Fernseher

Großpapa hat
einen Fernseher
in seiner Werkstatt.

Grandpa has
a television in his workshop.

tell*
sagen

Wilhelm sagte seinem
Hund, "Geh nach Hause."

William told his dog, "Go home."

teller
**der Kassierer
die Kassiererin**

Die Kassiererin
gab Thomas sein Geld.

The teller gave Thomas his money.

tennis
das Tennisspiel

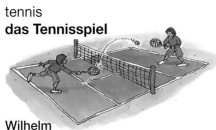

Wilhelm
und Stephan spielen Tennis.

William and Steven are playing tennis.

tennis racket
der Tennisschläger

Wilhelm
hält seinen
Tennisschläger.

William is holding his tennis racket.

tent
das Zelt

Die Mädchen
schliefen in einem großen Zelt.

The girls slept in a large tent.

tentacle
der Tentakel

Krakenarme
werden
Tentakel genannt.

Octopus arms are called tentacles.

terrible
schrecklich

Was
war
das für ein
schreckliches Geräusch?

What was that terrible noise?

than
als

Susanne ist
größer als
Jimmy.

Susan is bigger
than Jimmy.

thank you
vielen Dank

Vielen
Dank daß du "Bitte" sagtest.

Thank you for saying "please."

there
dort

Bitte leg
es dort hin.

Please put it there.

thermometer
das Thermometer

Das
Thermometer
zeigt an wie
heiß es ist.

The thermometer
shows how hot it is.

thin
dünn

Helene ist
zu dünn um
meinen Gürtel
zu tragen.

Helen is too thin
to wear my belt.

thing
das Ding

Was ist
das für
ein Ding?

What is this thing?

think*
denken

Stephan
denkt an
seinen Geburtstag.

Steven is thinking of his birthday.

thread
der Faden

Der Faden
geht durch
das Nadelöhr.

The thread goes
through the eye of the needle.

throne
der Thron

Der
König
und die
Königin sitzen
auf ihren Thronen.

The king and queen sit on their thrones.

through
durch

Wilhelm
ging durch
die Tür.

William walked
through the door.

throw*
werfen

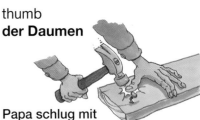

Wirf mir den
Basketball zu.

Throw the basketball to me.

thumb
der Daumen

Papa schlug mit
dem Hammer auf seinen Daumen.

Dad hit his thumb with the hammer.

ticket
die Eintrittskarte

Thomas hat eine
Eintrittskarte um
den Film zu sehen.

Thomas has a ticket
to see the movie.

tie
binden

Der Bauer
band den Bullen an den Zaun.
The farmer tied the bull to the fence.

tie
die Krawatte

Diese
Krawatte
ist für Papas
Geburtstag.
This tie is for Dad's birthday.

tiger
der Tiger

Tiger jagen
im Dschungel nach Nahrung.
Tigers hunt for food in the jungle.

tightrope
das Drahtseil

Unter dem
Drahtseil ist ein Netz.
There is a net under the tightrope.

time
die Zeit

Wieviel Zeit brauchst du?
How much time do you need?

tire
der Reifen

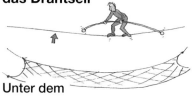

Die Reifen
dieses Traktors
sind so groß
wie mein Papa.
The tires on this
tractor are as tall as my dad.

to
zu

Es ist Zeit
zu Bett zu gehen.
It is time to go to bed.

toad
die Kröte

Diese
Kröte kann dir nicht wehtun.
This toad cannot hurt you.

toast
der Toast

Maria strich
Traubengelee
auf ihren Toast.
Mary spread grape jam on her toast.

toaster
der Toaster

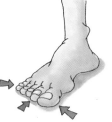

Unser Toaster hat
vier Öffnungen für Brot.
Our toaster has four holes for bread.

toe
die Zehe

Leute haben
fünf Zehen an jedem Fuß.
People have five toes on each foot.

together
zusammen

Susanne
und
Thomas
stehen
zusammen.
Susan and
Thomas are
standing
together.

toilet
die Toilette

Die Toilette
ist nahe dem
Waschbecken.
The toilet is near the sink.

tomato
die Tomate

Wilhelm
schnitt
eine Tomate
für den
Salat auf.
William cut up
a tomato for the salad.

tongue
die Zunge

Wilhelms
Zunge ist
purpur.
William's tongue is purple.

toolbox
der Werkzeugkasten

Der
Zimmermann
hat einen
Werkzeugkasten
in seinem Wagen.
The carpenter carries
a toolbox in his truck.

tooth*
der Zahn

Das Baby
hat seinen
ersten Zahn.
The baby has his first tooth.

toothbrush
die Zahnbürste

Der Zahnarzt
gab mir
eine neue
Zahnbürste.
The dentist
gave me a new toothbrush.

toothpaste
die Zahnpaste

Jimmy aß die Zahnpaste.
Jimmy was eating the toothpaste.

top
die Oberfläche

Ich verschüttete Marmelade
auf die Oberfläche des Tisches.
I spilled jam on the top of the table.

top
der Kreisel

Dieser Kreisel
dreht sich
sehr schnell.
This top is spinning very fast.

top hat
der Zylinder

Der Tänzer
trägt einen
Zylinder.
The dancer is
wearing a top hat.

tornado
der Tornado

Der Tornado
fegte durch die Stadt.
The tornado swept through the town.

towel
das Handtuch

Thomas
trocknete
das Geschirr
mit einem
alten Handtuch.
Thomas dried
the dishes with an old towel.

tower
der Turm

Das Schloß
hatte einen
Turm an
jeder Ecke.
The castle had
a tower at each corner.

town
die Stadt

Unsere Stadt ist sehr hübsch.
Our town is very pretty.

toy
das Spielzeug

Die Kinder
breiteten alle ihre Spielzeuge aus.
The children spread all their toys out.

toy store
der Spielzeugladen

Maria
kaufte eine
Puppe im
Spielzeugladen.
Mary bought a doll at the toy store.

tractor
der Traktor

Der Bauer
fuhr den
Traktor
ums Feld
herum.
The farmer drove
the tractor around the field.

traffic jam
der Verkehrsstau

In der
Stadt ist ein Verkehrsstau.
There is a traffic jam in the city.

traffic light
die Ampel

Halte an
wenn die
Ampel rot ist.
Stop when the
traffic light is red.

train
der Zug

Der Zug fuhr nicht rechtzeitig ab.
The train did not leave on time.

train station
der Bahnhof

Die
Passagiere
warteten auf
dem Bahnhof.
The passengers
waited at the train station.

trampoline
das Trampolin

Die Kinder
springen
auf und
ab auf dem
Trampolin.
The children jump up
and down on the trampoline.

trapeze
das Trapez

Susanne
hängt an
ihren Knien
vom Trapez.
Susan hangs
by her knees on the trapeze.

tray
das Tablett

Der Kellner
trug unser
Essen auf
einem Tablett.
The waiter carried
our food on a tray.

treasure
der Schatz

Stephan gräbt am Strande nach einem Schatz.

Steven is digging up treasure on the beach.

tree
der Baum

Neben der Kirche steht ein Baum.

There is a tree by the church.

tricycle
das Dreirad

Wessen Dreirad steht in der Einfahrt?

Whose tricycle is in the driveway?

trombone
die Posaune

Robert lehrt mich die Posaune zu spielen.

Robert is teaching me to play the trombone.

trophy
die Trophäe

Susanne gewann eine Trophäe dafür daß sie die Erste war.

Susan won a trophy for being first.

trousers
die Hosen

Papa trägt lange Hosen zur Arbeit.

Dad wears trousers to work.

truck
der Lastwagen

Der Lastwagen ist voller Kisten aus der Fabrik.

The truck is full of boxes from the factory.

trumpet
die Trompete

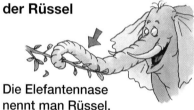

Der Musiklehrer gab Susanne eine Trompete.

The music teacher gave Susan a trumpet.

trunk
der Rüssel

Die Elefantennase nennt man Rüssel.

The elephant's nose is called a trunk.

trunk
der Kofferraum

Die Koffer sind in dem Kofferraum des Autos.

The suitcases are in the trunk of the car.

trunk
der Schließkoffer

Der Schließkoffer in der Dachstube enthält alte Kleider.

The trunk in the attic contains old clothing.

trunks
die Badehose

Roberts Badehose ist rot.

Robert's trunks are red.

tuba
die Tuba

Thomas sitzt auf einem Stuhl, um seine Tuba zu spielen.

Thomas sits on a chair to play his tuba.

tugboat
der Schlepper

Schlepper schieben das Schiff aus der Bucht.

Tugboats are pushing the ship out of the bay.

tuna
der Thunfisch

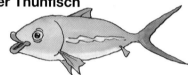

Der Thunfisch ist ein sehr großer Fisch.

The tuna is a very large fish.

turkey
der Truthahn

Der Truthahn ist ein sehr großer Vogel.

The turkey is a very large bird.

turtle
die Schildkröte

Schildkröten schwimmen im Teich.

Turtles swim in the pond.

tusk
der Stoßzahn

Ein Elefant hat zwei Stoßzähne.

An elephant has two tusks.

tuxedo
der Smoking

Mein Onkel trägt einen Smoking zum Tanz.

My uncle is wearing a tuxedo to the dance.

type
tippen

Maria lernt tippen.

Mary is learning to type.

typewriter
die Schreibmaschine

Die Sekretärin schreibt Briefe auf ihrer Schreibmaschine.

The secretary writes letters on her typewriter.

UuUuUuUu

umbrella
der Schirm

Stephan hielt den Schirm über uns.

Steven held the umbrella over us.

---

umpire
der Schiedsrichter

Der Schiedsrichter paßt sorgfältig auf.

The umpire watches carefully.

---

uncle
der Onkel

Helenes Onkel ist der Bruder ihrer Mutter.

Helen's uncle is her mother's brother.

---

under
unter

Jimmy ist unter dem Tisch.

Jimmy is under the table.

underwear
das Unterkleid

Stephans Mutter kaufte ihm neue Unterkleider.

Steven's mom bought him new underwear.

---

unicorn
das Einhorn

Das Einhorn hatte ein Horn auf seinem Kopf.

The unicorn had a horn on its head.

---

uniform
die Uniform

Polizisten und Polizistinnen tragen Uniformen.

Policemen and policewomen wear uniforms.

---

up
hinauf

Wilhelm sah zum Himmel hinauf.

William looked up at the sky.

---

use
benutzen

Susanne benutzt ihren Bleistift.

Susan is using her pencil.

use
die Anwendung

Sie bringt ihn zur guten Anwendung.

She is putting it to a good use.

VvVvVvVv

vacuum cleaner
der Staubsauger

Maria reinigt den Teppich mit dem Staubsauger.

Mary cleans the rug with the vacuum cleaner.

---

valley
das Tal

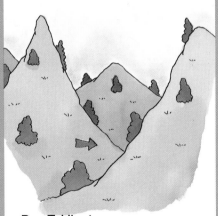

Das Tal liegt zwischen zwei Bergen.

The valley is between two mountains.

van
der Transporter

Die Mannschaft fährt zu dem Spiel in einem Transporter.
The team rides to the game in a van.

---

vase
die Vase
Auf dem Tisch steht eine Vase mit Blumen.
There is a vase of flowers on the table.

---

vegetable
das Gemüse

Erbsen, Spinat, und Kopfsalat sind grüne Gemüse.
Peas, spinach, and lettuce are green vegetables.

---

vegetable garden
der Gemüsegarten

Großmutter pflanzt einen Gemüsegarten.
Grandmother is planting a vegetable garden.

---

very
sehr

Wilhelm ist sehr müde.
William is very tired.

---

veterinarian
der Tierarzt
die Tierärztin

Der Tierarzt hilft kranken Tieren.
The veterinarian helps sick animals.

---

village
das Dorf

Susanne wohnt in einem kleinen Dorf nahe der Stadt.
Susan lives in a small village near the city.

---

violin
die Violine

Helene hält die Violine unter ihrem Kinn.
Helen holds the violin under her chin.

---

volleyball
das Volley-ballspiel

Wir spielten Volleyball am Strand.
We played volleyball on the beach.

WwWwWwWw

wade
waten

Thomas watet in dem Schwimmbecken.
Thomas is wading in the pool.

---

wagon
der Wagen

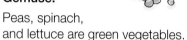

Helene zieht einen Wagen.
Helen is pulling a wagon.

---

waist
die Taille

Stephan hat einen Gürtel um seine Taille.
Steven has a belt around his waist.

---

wait
warten

Maria wartet auf den Bus.
Mary is waiting for the bus.

---

waiter
der Kellner

Der Kellner gab mir eine Speisekarte.
The waiter gave me a menu.

---

waiting room
das Wartezimmer

Das Wartezimmer ist voll.
The waiting room is full.

---

waitress
die Kellnerin

Die Kellnerin füllte mein Glas mit Wasser.
The waitress filled my glass with water.

---

walk
spazierengehen

Mutter geht spazieren, und die Kinder laufen.
Mother walks, and the children run.

wall
die Wand

Ein Bild hängt an der Wand.
A picture hangs on the wall.

---

wallet
die Brieftasche

Papa zog etwas Geld aus seiner Brieftasche.
Dad pulled some money out of his wallet.

---

walrus
das Walroß

Ein Walroß schwimmt in kaltem Wasser.
A walrus swims in cold water.

---

want
wollen

Willst du das lesen?
Do you want to read this?

---

warm
warm

Am Feuer ist es warm.
It is warm by the fire.

---

wash
waschen

Susanne wusch ihr Gesicht und ging ins Bett.
Susan washed her face and went to bed.

---

washing machine
die Waschmaschine

Marias Jeans sind in der Waschmaschine.
Mary's jeans are in the washing machine.

---

wasp
die Wespe

Wespen bauten ein Nest auf unserer Veranda.
Wasps built a nest on our porch.

---

wastebasket
der Abfalleimer

Großmama warf die Lumpen in den Abfalleimer.
Grandma threw the rags in the wastebasket.

---

watch
zuschauen

Ich schaue dem Fußballspiel im Fernsehen zu.
I watch the football game on television.

---

watch
die Armbanduhr

Robert gab Mama eine Armbanduhr zu ihrem Geburtstag.
Robert gave Mom a watch for her birthday.

---

water
das Wasser

Blumen brauchen Wasser um zu wachsen.
Flowers need water to grow.

water
gießen

Helene gießt die Blumen.
Helen is watering the flowers.

---

waterfall
der Wasserfall

Ein Wasserfall fließt von der Seite des Berges herab.
A waterfall comes down the side of the mountain.

---

watermelon
die Wassermelone

Tante Alice schnitt die Wassermelone auf.
Aunt Alice sliced the watermelon.

---

wave
winken

Maria winkte ihrem Vater zu.
Mary waved to her father.

---

wave
die Welle

Der Wind bläst den Ozean zu Wellen.
The wind blows the ocean into waves.

---

way
der Weg

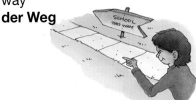

Das ist der Weg zur Schule.
This is the way to school.

---

wear*
tragen

Leute tragen Kleidung, aber Tiere tun es nicht.
People wear clothing, but animals do not.

weather
das Wetter

Das Wetter ändert sich oft.

The weather changes often.

---

wedding
die Hochzeit

Helene nahm an der Hochzeit ihrer Schwester Teil.

Helen was in her sister's wedding.

---

weed
jäten

Ich muß im Garten jäten!

I have to weed the garden!

weed
das Unkraut

In meinem Garten gibt es viel Unkraut.

There are many weeds in my garden.

---

week
die Woche

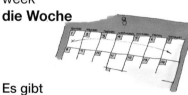

Es gibt sieben Tage in einer Woche.

There are seven days in a week.

---

welcome
willkommen

Wir hießen Wilhelm in unserem Hause willkommen.

We welcomed William to our house.

---

well
gut

Es geht Robert gut, und er ist gesund.

Robert is well and healthy.

---

well
der Brunnen

Die Jungen tranken Wasser vom Brunnen.

The boys drank water from the well.

---

wet
naß

Stephans Haar ist naß.

Steven's hair is wet.

---

whale
der Walfisch

Walfische sind sehr große Tiere.

Whales are very large animals.

---

what
was

Was ist das?

What is this?

---

wheat
der Weizen

Mehl wird aus Weizen hergestellt.

Flour is made from wheat.

---

wheel
das Rad

Mein Fahrrad hat zwei Räder.

My bicycle has two wheels.

---

wheelchair
der Rollstuhl

Tante Alice benutzt einen Rollstuhl.

Aunt Alice uses a wheelchair.

---

when
wann

Wann wird der Wecker klingeln?

When will the alarm clock ring?

---

where
wo

Wo sind Susannes Schuhe?

Where are Susan's shoes?

---

whistle
die Pfeife

Sie alle bliesen ihre Pfeifen!

They all blew their whistles!

---

white
weiß

Schneeflocken sind weiß.

Snowflakes are white.

wide
breit

Der Fluß ist sehr breit.
The river is very wide.

wig
die Perücke

Der Clown trägt
eine komische
orange Perücke.
The clown wears
a silly orange wig.

win*
gewinnen

Helene
gewann
einen Preis.
Helen won a prize.

wind
der Wind

Der Wind
blies meinen Hut weg.
The wind blew my hat off.

window
das Fenster

Im Sommer sind
die Fenster offen.
The windows are
open in the summer.

wing
der
Flügel

Vögel
benutzen
ihre Flügel
zum Fliegen.
Birds use their wings to fly.

---

winter
der Winter

Schnee
bedeckt den Hof im Winter.
Snow covers the yard in winter.

wipe
wischen

Susanne
wischt
das Wasser
von ihrer Brille.
Susan is wiping
the water off her glasses.

with
mit

Maria traf
den Nagel
mit einem Hammer.
Mary hit the nail with a hammer.

wolf*
der Wolf

Ein Wolf
lief aus dem Wald heraus.
A wolf ran out of the forest.

woman*
die Frau

Meine Tante
ist eine
kleine Frau.
My aunt is a
short woman.

wood
das Holz

Robert schlug
mehr Holz für
den Kamin.
Robert cut more
wood for the fireplace.

---

woodpecker
der Specht

Ein Specht
macht Löcher
in die Bäume.
A woodpecker
makes holes in trees.

word
das Wort

Maria las die
Wörter auf der Tafel.
Mary read the words
on the chalkboard.

work
arbeiten

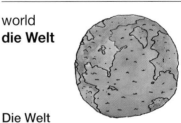

Wir alle
arbeiten
in der Schule.
We all work at school.

workshop
die
Werkstatt

Papa
repariert
Sachen in seiner Werkstatt.
Dad fixes things in his workshop.

world
die Welt

Die Welt
ist rund wie ein Ball.
The world is round like a ball.

worm
der Wurm

Der Vogel
fand einen Wurm im Gras.
The bird found a worm in the grass.

wreath
der Kranz

An unserer Tür hängt ein Kranz.

There is a wreath on our door.

wrench
der Schrauben-schlüssel

Papa reparierte den Wasserhahn mit einem Schraubenschlüssel.

Dad fixed the faucet with a wrench.

wrestling
der Ringkampf

Robert ist in der Ringkampf-Mannschaft.

Robert is on the wrestling team.

wrinkles
die Falten

Stephans Hosen sind voller Falten.

Steven's pants are full of wrinkles.

wrist
das Handgelenk

Susanne hat einen Verband an ihrem Handgelenk.

Susan has a bandage on her wrist.

write*
schreiben

Einige Flugzeuge schreiben am Himmel.

Some airplanes write in the sky.

XxXxXxXx

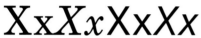

xylophone
das Xylophon

Helene spielt Xylophon.

Helen plays the xylophone.

ZzZzZzZz

zebra
das Zebra

Ein Zebra hat schwarze und weiße Streifen.

A zebra has black and white stripes.

zipper
der Reißverschluß

Stephans Jacke hat einen langen Reißverschluß.

Steven's jacket has a long zipper.

zoo
der Zoo

Der Zoo ist mein Lieblingsplatz.

The zoo is my favorite place.

YyYyYyYy

yarn
das Garn

Das Kätzchen spielt gern mit Garn.

The kitten loves to play with yarn.

yellow
gelb

Der Schulbus ist gelb.

The school bus is yellow.

yolk
das Dotter

Ein Dotter ist der gelbe Teil eines Eies.

A yolk is the yellow part of an egg.

yard
der Hof

Um den Hof ist ein Zaun.

The yard has a fence around it.

Appendices

Numbers
Die Nummern

Days of the Week
Die Wochentage

Months of the Year
Die Monaten

Shapes
Die Formen

Directions
Die Richtungen

Time
Die Uhrzeiten

Irregular English Verbs,
Nouns, and Adjectives

Numbers
Die Nummern

0	**½**	**1**	**2**	**3**	**4**	**5**	**6**	**7**	**8**
zero	one-half	one	two	three	four	five	six	seven	eight
null	**ein halb**	**eins**	**zwei**	**drei**	**vier**	**fünf**	**sechs**	**sieben**	**acht**

9	**10**	**11**	**12**	**13**	**14**	**15**	**16**
nine	ten	eleven	twelve	thirteen	fourteen	fifteen	sixteen
neun	**zehn**	**elf**	**zwölf**	**dreizehn**	**vierzehn**	**fünfzehn**	**sechzehn**

17	**18**	**19**	**20**	**21**	**22**	**23**
seventeen	eighteen	nineteen	twenty	twenty-one	twenty-two	twenty-three
siebzehn	**achtzehn**	**neunzehn**	**zwanzig**	**einundzwanzig**	**zweiundzwanzig**	**dreiundzwanzig**

24	**25**	**26**	**27**	**28**	**29**
twenty-four	twenty-five	twenty-six	twenty-seven	twenty-eight	twenty-nine
vierundzwanzig	**fünfundzwanzig**	**sechsundzwanzig**	**siebenundzwanzig**	**achtundzwanzig**	**neunundzwanzig**

30	**31**	**32**	**33**	**34**
thirty	thirty-one	thirty-two	thirty-three	thirty-four
dreißig	**einunddreißig**	**zweiunddreißig**	**dreiunddreißig**	**vierunddreißig**

35	**36**	**37**	**38**	**39**
thirty-five	thirty-six	thirty-seven	thirty-eight	thirty-nine
fünfunddreißig	**sechsunddreißig**	**siebenunddreißig**	**achtunddreißig**	**neununddreißig**

40	**41**	**42**	**43**	**44**
forty	forty-one	forty-two	forty-three	forty-four
vierzig	**einundvierzig**	**zweiundvierzig**	**dreiundvierzig**	**vierundvierzig**

45	**46**	**47**	**48**	**49**
forty-five	forty-six	forty-seven	forty-eight	forty-nine
fünfundvierzig	**sechsundvierzig**	**siebenundvierzig**	**achtundvierzig**	**neunundvierzig**

50	**51**	**52**	**53**	**54**
fifty	fifty-one	fifty-two	fifty-three	fifty-four
fünfzig	**einundfünfzig**	**zweiundfünfzig**	**dreiundfünfzig**	**vierundfünfzig**

55	**56**	**57**	**58**	**59**
fifty-five	fifty-six	fifty-seven	fifty-eight	fifty-nine
fünfundfünfzig	**sechsundfünfzig**	**siebenundfünfzig**	**achtundfünfzig**	**neunundfünfzig**

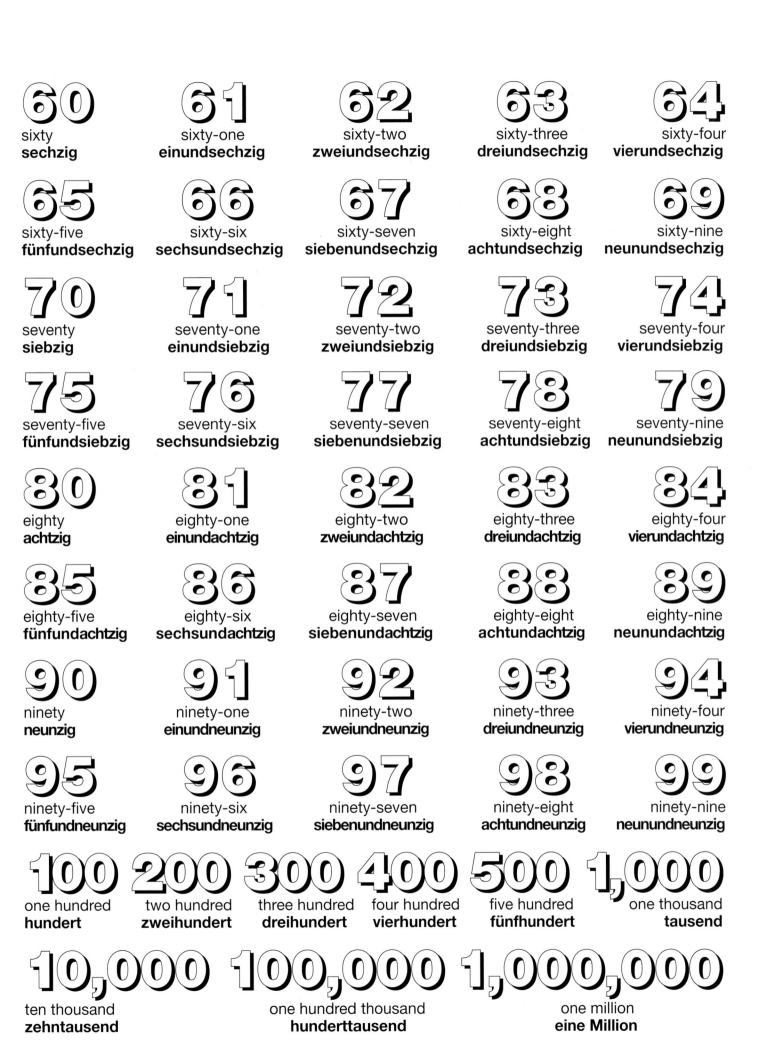

60	61	62	63	64
sixty **sechzig**	sixty-one **einundsechzig**	sixty-two **zweiundsechzig**	sixty-three **dreiundsechzig**	sixty-four **vierundsechzig**
65	66	67	68	69
sixty-five **fünfundsechzig**	sixty-six **sechsundsechzig**	sixty-seven **siebenundsechzig**	sixty-eight **achtundsechzig**	sixty-nine **neunundsechzig**
70	71	72	73	74
seventy **siebzig**	seventy-one **einundsiebzig**	seventy-two **zweiundsiebzig**	seventy-three **dreiundsiebzig**	seventy-four **vierundsiebzig**
75	76	77	78	79
seventy-five **fünfundsiebzig**	seventy-six **sechsundsiebzig**	seventy-seven **siebenundsiebzig**	seventy-eight **achtundsiebzig**	seventy-nine **neunundsiebzig**
80	81	82	83	84
eighty **achtzig**	eighty-one **einundachtzig**	eighty-two **zweiundachtzig**	eighty-three **dreiundachtzig**	eighty-four **vierundachtzig**
85	86	87	88	89
eighty-five **fünfundachtzig**	eighty-six **sechsundachtzig**	eighty-seven **siebenundachtzig**	eighty-eight **achtundachtzig**	eighty-nine **neunundachtzig**
90	91	92	93	94
ninety **neunzig**	ninety-one **einundneunzig**	ninety-two **zweiundneunzig**	ninety-three **dreiundneunzig**	ninety-four **vierundneunzig**
95	96	97	98	99
ninety-five **fünfundneunzig**	ninety-six **sechsundneunzig**	ninety-seven **siebenundneunzig**	ninety-eight **achtundneunzig**	ninety-nine **neunundneunzig**

100	200	300	400	500	1,000
one hundred **hundert**	two hundred **zweihundert**	three hundred **dreihundert**	four hundred **vierhundert**	five hundred **fünfhundert**	one thousand **tausend**

10,000	100,000	1,000,000
ten thousand **zehntausend**	one hundred thousand **hunderttausend**	one million **eine Million**

Days of the Week
Die Wochentage

Monday

der
Montag

Tuesday

der
Dienstag

Wednesday

der
Mittwoch

Thursday

der
Donnerstag

Friday

der
Freitag

Saturday

der
Samstag,
Sonnabend

Sunday

der
Sonntag

Months of the Year
Die Monaten

January
der
Januar

February
der
Februar

March
der März

April
der April

May
der Mai

June
der Juni

July
der Juli

August
der
August

September
der
September

October
der
Oktober

November
der
November

December
der
Dezember

Shapes
Die Formen

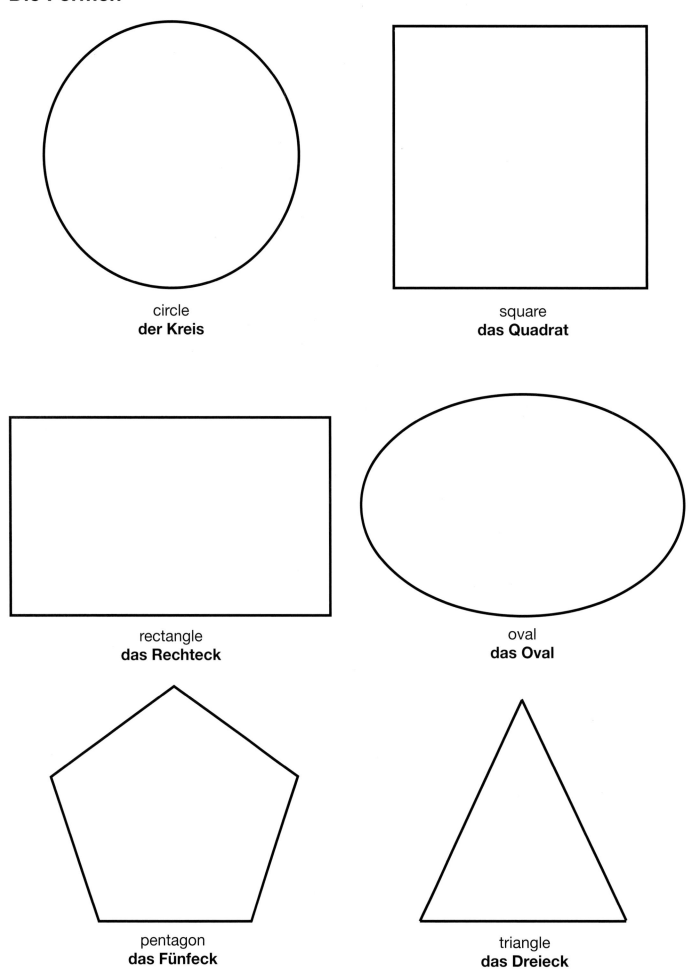

circle
der Kreis

square
das Quadrat

rectangle
das Rechteck

oval
das Oval

pentagon
das Fünfeck

triangle
das Dreieck

Directions
Die Richtungen

North
der Norden

Northwest
der Nordwesten

South
der Süden

Southwest
der Südwesten

East
der Osten

Northeast
der Nordosten

West
der Westen

Southeast
der Südosten

Time
Die Uhrzeiten

It is half past six.
Es ist halb sieben.

It is noon.
Es ist der Mittag.

It is midnight.
Es ist die Mitternacht.

It is six o'clock.
Es ist sechs Uhr.

It is a quarter of two.
Es ist viertel vor zwei.

It is 1:00 P.M.
Es ist ein Uhr nachmittags.

It is 1:00 A.M.
Es ist ein Uhr morgens.

Irregular English Verbs

become, became, become
bite, bit, bitten
blow, blew, blown
break, broke, broken
build, built, built
burn, burned or burnt, burned
buy, bought, bought
catch, caught, caught
come, came, come
cut, cut, cut
dig, dug, dug
do, did, done
draw, drew, drawn
dream, dreamt or dreamed, dreamt or
   dreamed
drink, drank, drunk
drive, drove, driven
eat, ate, eaten
fall, fell, fallen
find, found, found
fly, flew, flown
forget, forgot, forgotten
freeze, froze, frozen
give, gave, given
go, went, gone
grow, grew, grown
hang, hung, hung
have, had, had
hit, hit, hit
hold, held, held
hurt, hurt, hurt
is, was, been (be)

keep, kept, kept
knit, knit or knitted, knit or knitted
leap, leapt or leaped, leapt or leaped
light, lighted or lit, lighted or lit
make, made, made
put, put, put
read, read, read
ride, rode, ridden
ring, rang, rung
run, ran, run
see, saw, seen
sell, sold, sold
sew, sewed, sewn
show, showed, shown
sing, sang, sung
sit, sat, sat
sleep, slept, slept
slide, slid, slid
speak, spoke, spoken
spin, spun, spun
spread, spread, spread
stand, stood, stood
sweep, swept, swept
swim, swam, swum
take, took, taken
teach, taught, taught
tell, told, told
think, thought, thought
throw, threw, thrown
wear, wore, worn
win, won, won
write, wrote, written

Irregular English Nouns

calf, calves
child, children
deer, deer
die, dice
doorman, doormen
fish, fish or fishes
fisherman, fishermen
foot, feet
goose, geese
half, halves
handkerchief, handkerchiefs
   or handkerchieves
hoof, hooves
knife, knives
leaf, leaves
man, men
mouse, mice
policeman, policemen
policewoman, policewomen
scarf, scarves
sheep, sheep
shelf, shelves
snowman, snowmen
starfish, starfish
tooth, teeth
wolf, wolves
woman, women

Irregular English Adjectives

good, better, best
less, least
more, most

Index

Busch, der bush 13
Butter, die butter 13
Butterbrot, das sandwich 60

C

Clown, der clown 18
Computer, der computer 19
Cousin, der cousin 20
Cousine, die cousin 20
Cowboy, der cowboy 20

D

Dach, das roof 58
Dachstube, die attic 6
Damespiel, das checkers 16
Datum, das date 22
Daumen, der thumb 71
Deck, das deck 22
Decke, die ceiling 16
Decken, die covers 20
Delphin, der dolphin 24
denken think* 71
dick fat 28
Ding, das thing 71
Dinosaurier, der dinosaur 23
Dock, das dock 23
Dollar, der dollar 24
Dorf, das village 76
dort there 71
Dose, die can 14
Dotter, das yolk 80
Drache, der dragon 24
Drache, der kite 40
Drahtseil, das tightrope 72
drehen spin* 66
Dreirad, das tricycle 74
drücken squeeze 66
Dschungel, der jungle 39
dumm foolish 30
dunkel dark 22
dünn thin 71
durch through 71
Dusche, die shower 62
Dutzend, das dozen 24

E

Ecke, die corner 19
Ei, das egg 26
Eichel, die acorn 4
Eichhörnchen, das squirrel 66
Eidechse, die lizard 43
Eimer, der bucket 13
Eimer, der pail 50
einfach plain 53
Einfahrt, die driveway 25
Eingang, der entrance 26
Einhorn, das unicorn 75
einige some 65
einkaufen shop 62

Eintrittskarte, die ticket 71
Eis, das ice 38
Eisbär, der polar bear 54
Eiscreme, die ice cream 38
Eiszapfen, der icicle 38
Elefant, der elephant 26
Ellbogen, der elbow 26
Eltern, die parents 50
Ende, das end 26
Engel, der angel 5
Entchen, das duckling 25
Ente, die duck 25
enthalten contain 19
Erbse, die pea 51
Erdbeere, die strawberry 68
Erde, die Earth 26
Erdnuß, die peanut 51
Ernte, die crop 20
erröten blush 11
Esel, der donkey 24
essen eat* 26
Essen, das food 30
Eßzimmer, das dining room 23
Etikett, das label 40
Eule, die owl 49
Examen, das exam 27

F

Fabrik, die factory 27
Faden, der thread 71
Fahne, die banner 7
Fahne, die flag 29
fahren drive* 25
fahren ride* 57
Fahrrad, das bicycle 9
fallen fall* 27
fallen lassen drop 25
Fallschirm, der parachute 50
Falten, die wrinkles 80
Familie, die family 27
fangen catch* 15
Farbe, die color 18
Farbe, die paint 50
Farn, der fern 28
Faß, das barrel 7
faul lazy 41
Fausthandschuhe, die mittens 45
Feder, die feather 28
Federballspiel, das badminton 6
Fee, die fairy 27
Feier, die party 51
Feld, das field 28
Felsblock, der boulder 11
Fenster, das window 79
Fernglas, das binoculars 10
Fernseher, der television 70
Feuer, das fire 29
Feuerwehr, die fire engine 29
Feuerwehrmann, der fire fighter 29
Fieber, das fever 28

Film, der movie 46
finden find* 28
Finger, der finger 28
Fingernagel, der fingernail 28
Fisch, der fish* 29
fischen fish 29
Fischer, der fisherman* 29
flach flat 29
Flachland, das plain 53
Flamingo, der flamingo 29
Flamme, die flame 29
Flasche, die bottle 11
Fleck, der spot 66
Fledermaus, die bat 8
Fleisch, das meat 44
Fliege, die fly 30
fliegen fly* 30
Flosse, die fin 28
Flöte, die flute 30
Flügel, der wing 79
Flugzeug, das airplane 4
Fluß, der river 58
folgen follow 30
Foto, das photograph 52
Frau, die woman* 79
Freund, der friend 31
Freundin, die friend 31
frieren freeze* 31
Friseur, der barber 7
froh glad 32
Frosch, der frog 31
Frost, der frost 31
früh early 26
Frühling, der spring 66
Frühstück, das breakfast 12
Fuchs, der fox 31
füllen fill 28
Füllen, das colt 18
Füllhalter, der pen 51
Fuß, der foot* 30
Fußballspiel, das football 30
Fußbank, die footstool 30
Fußboden, der floor 30
Füße, die feet* 28
Fußspur, die footprint 30

G

Gabel, die fork 31
Gans, die goose* 33
Gänschen, das gosling 33
Gänseblümchen, das daisy 22
ganz completely 19
Garage, die garage 32
Garn, das yarn 80
Garten, der garden 32
Gartenschlauch, der garden hose 32
Gärtner, der gardener 32
Gas, das gas 32
Gast, der guest 34
Gebäude, das building 13

geben give* 32
Geburtstag, der birthday 10
Geburtstagskuchen, der birthday cake 10
Gefriertruhe, die freezer 31
gehen go* 33
Geist, der ghost 32
gelb yellow 80
Geld, das money 45
Gelee, das jelly 38
Gemüse, das vegetable 76
Gemüsegarten, der vegetable garden 76
Gepäck, das baggage 6
Geruch, der smell 64
Geschenk, das gift 32
Geschenk, das present 55
Geschirr, das dishes 23
Geschmack, der flavor 29
Gesicht, das face 27
gesund healthy 35
Getränk, das drink 25
Gewächshaus, das greenhouse 34
gewinnen win* 79
gießen water 77
Gipsverband, der cast 15
Giraffe, die giraffe 32
Gitarre, die guitar 34
Glas, das glass 32
glatt straight (hair) 68
gleich alike 4
Globus, der globe 33
glücklich happy 35
Glühbirne, die lightbulb 42
golden gold 33
Gorilla, der gorilla 33
graben dig* 23
Gras, das grass 34
grau gray 34
Grill, der barbecue 7
grillen barbecue 7
Grippe, die flu 30
groß big 10
groß large 41
Größe, die size 63
Großeltern, die grandparents 33
Großmutter, die grandmother 33
Großpapa, der grandpa 33
Großvater, der grandfather 33
grün green 34
Gruppe, die group 34
Gurke, die cucumber 21
Gürtel, der belt 9
gut good* 33
gut well 78
gutaussehend handsome 35

H

Haar, das hair 34
haben have* 35

Hacke, die hoe 36
hacken hoe 36
Hahn, der rooster 58
Haifisch, der shark 61
halb half* 34
Hals, der neck 47
Halsband, das collar 18
halten hold* 36
halten stop 68
Haltezeichen, das stop sign 68
Hamburger, der hamburger 34
Hammer, der hammer 34
hämmern hammer 34
Hand, die hand 35
Handgelenk, das wrist 80
Handlungen, die actions 4
Handschuh, der glove 33
Handtuch, das towel 73
Hängematte, die hammock 35
hängen hang* 35
Harfe, die harp 35
Harke, die rake 56
hart hard 35
Haufen, der pile 53
Haus, das house 37
Hausaufgabe, die homework 36
Häuserblock, der block 10
Haustier, das pet 52
heben lift 42
Heftklammern, die staples 67
Heftmaschine, die stapler 67
Heim, das home 36
heiß hot 37
Heizung, die furnace 31
helfen help 36
Hemd, das shirt 62
Henne, die hen 36
herab off 48
Herbst, der autumn 6
Herbst, der fall 27
Herd, der stove 68
Herde, die herd 36
Herz, das heart 35
Heu, das hay 35
Heuschrecke, die grasshopper 34
hierhin here 36
Himbeeren, die raspberries 56
Himmel, der sky 63
hinab down 24
hinauf up 75
hinaufsteigen climb 17
hinter behind 9
hitze, die heat 35
hoch high 36
hoch tall 70
Hochzeit, die wedding 78
Höcker, der hump 37
Hockeyspiel, das hockey 36
Hof, der yard 80
Höhle, die cave 15
Holz, das wood 79

Holzscheit, das log 43
Honig, der honey 36
Horn, das horn 37
Hosen, die pants 50
Hosen, die trousers 74
Hotel, das hotel 37
Hubschrauber, der helicopter 36
Huf, der hoof* 37
Hügel, der hill 36
Huhn, das chicken 16
Hummer, der lobster 43
Hund, der dog 23
Hündchen, das puppy 55
hungrig hungry 37
husten cough 20
Hut, der hat 35

I

Imbiß, der snack 64
immer always 4
in into 38
Insekt, das insect 38
Insel, die island 38

J

Jacke, die jacket 38
jäten weed 78
Jeans, die jeans 38
jede each 25
jedes every 27
Jeep, der jeep 38
Jet, der jet 39
joggen jog 39
jonglieren juggle 39
Junge, der boy 12
Juwel, das jewel 39
Juwelier, der jeweler 39

K

Kaffee, der coffee 18
Käfig, der cage 14
Kalb, das calf* 14
Kalender, der calendar 14
kalt cold 18
Kamel, das camel 14
Kamin, der fireplace 29
Kamm, der comb 18
Kanal, der canal 14
Känguruh, das kangaroo 39
Kaninchen, das rabbit 56
Kanu, das canoe 14
Kapelle, die band 7
Kapuze, die hood 37
Kardinal, der cardinal 15
Karikatur, die cartoon 15
Karre, die cart 15
Karten, die cards 15
Kartoffel, die potato 55

Kartoffelchips, die potato chips 55

Käse, der cheese 16

Kassierer, der cashier 15

Kassierer, der teller 70

Kassiererin, die cashier 15

Kassiererin, die teller 70

Kätzchen, das kitten 40

Katze, die cat 15

kaufen buy* 13

Kaulquappe, die tadpole 70

kehren sweep* 69

Kehrschaufel, die dustpan 25

Kellner, der waiter 76

Kellnerin, die waitress 76

Kerze, die candle 14

Kessel, der kettle 39

Ketchup, das ketchup 39

Kette, die necklace 47

Kiemen, die gills 32

Kind, das child* 16

Kinder, die children* 16

Kinderwagen, der stroller 68

Kinn, das chin 17

Kirche, die church 17

Kirsche, die cherry 16

Kissen, das pillow 53

Kiste, die crate 20

klar clear 17

Klarinette, die clarinet 17

Klassenzimmer, das classroom 17

klatschen clap 17

Klaue, die claw 17

kleben paste 51

Klebstoff, der paste 51

Kleid, das dress 24

Kleiderbügel, der hanger 35

Kleidung, die clothes 18

Kleidung, die clothing 18

klein little 43

klein short 62

klein small 64

Kleingeld, das change 16

Klempner, der plumber 54

Klettergerüst, das jungle gym 39

Klingel, die bell 9

knabbern bite* 10

Knall, der bang 7

Knie, das knee 40

Knochen, der bone 11

Knopf, der button 13

Knoten, der knot 40

Koch, der cook 19

kochen cook 19

Koffer, der suitcase 69

Kofferraum, der trunk 74

Kohl, der cabbage 14

Komet, der comet 19

komisch silly 63

kommen come* 19

Kommode, die dresser 25

Kompaß, der compass 19

König, der king 40

Königin, die queen 56

Kopf, der head 35

Kopfsprung, der dive 23

Korb, der basket 8

Körper, der body 11

köstlich delicious 22

Kostüm, das costume 19

Koyote, der coyote 20

Kräcker, der cracker 20

Krake, der octopus 48

Kran, der crane 20

Kranich, der crane 20

krank sick 62

Krankenhaus, das hospital 37

Krankenschwester, die nurse 48

Krankenwagen, der ambulance 5

Kranz, der wreath 80

Krawatte, die necktie 47

Krawatte, die tie 72

Kreide, die chalk 16

Kreis, der circle 17

Kreisel, der top 73

Krokodil, das crocodile 20

Krone, die crown 21

Kröte, die toad 72

Krücke, die crutch 21

Krug, der pitcher 53

Kruste, die crust 21

Küche, die kitchen 40

Kuchen, der cake 14

Kücken, das chick 16

Kuh, die cow 20

kühl cool 19

Kühlschrank, der refrigerator 57

Kunst, die art 5

Künstler, der artist 5

Künstlerin, die artist 5

Kürbis, der pumpkin 55

Kurve, die curve 21

L

lächeln smile 64

Lächeln, das smile 64

lachen laugh 41

Lachen, das laugh 41

Laden, der shop 62

Lager, das camp 14

Lamm, das lamb 41

Lampe, die lamp 41

Landkarte, die map 44

lang long 43

langsam slow 64

langweilig dull 25

Lappen, der rag 56

Lärm, der noise 48

Lastwagen, der truck 74

laufen run* 59

Läufer, der runner 59

Läuferin, die runner 59

laut loud 43

läuten ring* 57

Lebensmittelgeschäft, das grocery store 34

lecken lick 42

Leder, das leather 41

leer empty 26

legen put* 56

Lehm, der clay 17

lehren teach* 70

Lehrer, der teacher 70

Lehrerin, die teacher 70

leicht easy 26

Leim, der glue 33

leimen glue 33

Leiter, die ladder 40

Leopard, der leopard 42

lernen learn 41

lesen read* 57

letzt last 41

Leute, die people 52

lieben love 43

liebsten, am favorite 28

Limonade, die lemonade 42

Limonade, die soft drink 65

Limone, die lime 42

Lineal, das ruler 59

link left 41

Lippe, die lip 43

Liste, die list 43

Loch, das hole 36

lockig curly 21

Löffel, der spoon 66

Löwe, der lion 43

Löwenzahn, der dandelion 22

Luft, die air 4

Lutscher, der lollipop 43

M

machen make* 44

Mädchen, das girl 32

Magnet, der magnet 44

Mahl, das meal 44

Mähne, die mane 44

Mais, der corn 19

malen paint 50

Malpinsel, der paintbrush 50

Mama, die mom 45

Mann, der man* 44

Mannschaft, die team 70

Mantel, der coat 18

Marmelade, die jam 38

Maske, die mask 44

Matrose, der sailor 59

Maus, die mouse* 46

Mechaniker, der mechanic 45

Medaille, die medal 45

Medizin, die medicine 45

Meer, das sea 61

Mehl, das flour 29

mehr more* 46

Melone, die melon 45
Menschenmenge, die crowd 20
Messer, das knife* 40
Mikrofon, das microphone 45
Mikroskop, das microscope 45
Milch, die milk 45
mischen mix 45
mit with 79
Mittag, der noon 48
Mittagessen, das lunch 43
mittelgroß medium 45
Möbel, die furniture 31
mögen like 42
Möhre, die carrot 15
Monat, der month 46
Mond, der moon 46
Morgen, der morning 46
Morgenmantel, der robe 58
Motor, der engine 26
Motte, die moth 46
Mücke, die mosquito 46
Mund, der mouth 46
Münze, die coin 18
Muschel, die seashell 61
Museum, das museum 46
Musik, die music 46
Müsli, das cereal 16
Mutter, die mother 46
Mütze, die cap 14

N

nach after 4
Nacht, die night 48
Nachtisch, der dessert 23
Nadel, die needle 47
Nadel, die pin 53
Nagel, der nail 47
nageln nail 47
nahe close 18
nahe near 47
nähen sew* 61
Nähmaschine, die sewing machine 61
Name, der name 47
Nase, die nose 48
Nashorn, das rhinoceros 57
naß wet 78
Nebel, der fog 30
neben beside 9
nehmen take* 70
Nest, das nest 47
Netz, das net 47
neu new 47
Nickerchen, das nap 47
niedlich cute 21
niemals never 47
niesen sneeze 64
Nilpferd, das hippopotamus 36
Note, die bill 10
Notiz, die note 48
Notizblock, der notepad 48

Nudeln, die noodles 48
Nummer, die number 48
Nuß, die nut 48

O

Oberfläche, die top 73
Obst, das fruit 31
Ofen, der oven 49
offen open 49
öffnen open 49
oft often 49
Ohr, das ear 26
Ohrenschützer, die earmuffs 26
Ohrring, der earring 26
Öl, das oil 49
Omelett, das omelet 49
Onkel, der uncle 75
orange orange 49
Orchester, das orchestra 49
Ozean, der ocean 48

P

Paket, das package 50
Palast, der palace 50
Pampelmuse, die grapefruit 33
Panda, der panda 50
Papa, der dad 22
Papagei, der parrot 51
Papier, das paper 50
Parade, die parade 50
Park, der park 50
Passagier, der passenger 51
Patient, der patient 51
Pelz, der fur 31
Person, die person 52
Perücke, die wig 79
Pfad, der path 51
Pfanne, die pan 50
Pfeffer, der pepper 52
Pfeife, die whistle 78
Pfeil, der arrow 5
Pfeilspitze, die arrowhead 5
Pferd, das horse 37
Pferdeschwanz, der ponytail 54
Pfirsich, der peach 51
Pflanze, die plant 53
pflanzen plant 53
Pförtner, der doorman* 24
Pfote, die paw 51
Pfütze, die puddle 55
Phantasie, die make-believe 44
Piano, das piano 52
Picknick, das picnic 52
Pille, die pill 53
Pilot, der pilot 53
Pilz, der mushroom 46
Pinguin, der penguin 52
Planet, der planet 53
Platz, der place 53
Platz, der space 65

Plätzchen, das cookie 19
Polizei, die police 54
Polizeiauto, das police car 54
Polizist, der policeman* 54
Polizistin, die policewoman* 54
Pommes Frites, die french fries 31
Ponyhaare, die bangs 7
Popcorn, das popcorn 54
Posaune, die trombone 74
Post, die mail 44
Postamt, das post office 54
Preis, der price 55
Preis, der prize 55
Prinz, der prince 55
Prinzessin, die princess 55
pudern powder 55
Pullover, der sweater 69
Pult, das desk 22
Puppe, die doll 24
Puppe, die puppet 55
Puppenhaus, das dollhouse 24
purpur purple 55
Purzelbaum, der somersault 65
putzen clean 17
Puzzlespiel, das jigsaw puzzle 39
Pyjamas, die pajamas 50

Q

Quadrat, das square 66

R

Rad, das wheel 78
Radiergummi, das eraser 27
Radio, das radio 56
Ranch, die ranch 56
Rasen, der lawn 41
Rasenmäher, der lawn mower 41
Rätsel, das puzzle 56
Ratte, die rat 57
Rauch, der smoke 64
Raumschiff, das spaceship 65
Raupe, die caterpillar 15
recht right 57
Regal, das shelf* 62
Regen, der rain 56
Regenbogen, der rainbow 56
Regenmantel, der raincoat 56
Reh, das deer* 22
reiben rub 59
Reifen, der hoop 37
Reifen, der tire 72
Reihe, die line 43
Reis, der rice 57
Reißverschluß, der zipper 80
rennen race 56
reparieren fix 29
Reporter, der reporter 57
Reptil, das reptile 57
Restaurant, das restaurant 57
richtig right 57

riechen smell 64
Ring, der ring 57
Ringkampf, der wrestling 80
Rock, der skirt 63
rollen roll 58
Rollschuhbrett, das skateboard 63
Rollschuhe, die roller skates 58
Rollstuhl, der wheelchair 78
rosa pink 53
Rose, die rose 58
rot red 57
Rotkehlchen, das robin 58
Rucksack, der backpack 6
Rückseite, die back 6
Ruder, das oar 48
Ruderboot, das rowboat 58
ruhig quiet 56
rund round 58
Rüssel, der trunk 74
rutschen slide* 64

S

Saat, die seed 61
Sack, der sack 59
Saft, der juice 39
sägen saw 60
sagen tell* 70
Sahne, die cream 20
Salat, der salad 59
Salz, der salt 59
Sand, der sand 59
Sandalen, die sandals 60
Sandkiste, die sandbox 60
Sänger, der singer 63
Sängerin, die singer 63
Sanitäter, der paramedic 50
Sattel, der saddle 59
sauber clean 17
Saxophon, das saxophone 60
Schachtel, die box 12
Schaf, das sheep* 61
Schal, der scarf* 60
scharf sharp 61
Schatten, der shadow 61
Schatz, der treasure 74
Schaufel, die shovel 62
Schaukel, die swing 69
schaukeln rock 58
schaukeln swing 69
Schauspieler, der actor 4
Schauspielerin, die actress 4
Scheck, der check 16
scheiben push 56
Scheinwerfer, der spotlight 66
Schere, die scissors 60
Scheune, die barn 7
Schiedsrichter, der umpire 75
Schiff, das ship 62
Schiffswrack, das shipwreck 62
Schild, das sign 63
Schildkröte, die turtle 74

Schinken, der ham 34
Schirm, der umbrella 75
schlafen sleep* 64
Schlafzimmer, das bedroom 9
schlagen hit* 36
Schläger, der bat 8
Schlamm, der mud 46
Schlange, die snake 64
Schlauch, der hose 37
schlecht bad 6
Schleife, die bow 11
Schleife, die ribbon 57
Schlepper, der tugboat 74
schließen close 18
Schließkoffer, der trunk 74
Schlitten, der sled 64
Schlittschuh, der ice skate 38
Schlittschuh laufen skate 63
Schloß, das castle 15
Schloß, das lock 43
schlummern nap 47
Schlüssel, der key 39
schmal narrow 47
schmelzen melt 45
Schmerz, der pain 50
Schmetterling, der butterfly 13
Schmutz, der dirt 23
schmutzig dirty 23
Schnabel, der beak 8
Schnabel, der bill 10
Schnalle, die buckle 13
Schnecke, die snail 64
Schnee, der snow 64
Schneeball, der snowball 64
Schneeflocke, die snowflake 64
Schneemann, der snowman* 65
Schneesturm, der snowstorm 65
schneiden cut* 21
schnell fast 28
schnitzen carve 15
Schnur, die string 68
Schnürband, das shoelace 62
Schnurrbart, der mustache 46
Schokolade, die chocolate 17
schön beautiful 9
schön pretty 55
Schornstein, der chimney 17
Schoß, der lap 41
Schrank, der closet 18
Schrank, der cupboard 21
Schraube, die screw 60
Schraubenschlüssel, der wrench 80
Schraubenzieher, der screwdriver 60
schrecklich terrible 71
schreiben write* 80
Schreibmaschine, die typewriter 75
Schublade, die drawer 24
Schuh, der shoe 62
Schulbus, der school bus 60

Schule, die school 60
Schüler, der student 68
Schulklasse, die class 17
Schulter, die shoulder 62
Schuppe, die scale 60
Schürze, die apron 5
Schüssel, die bowl 11
Schutzbrille, die goggles 33
schwach dim 23
Schwamm, der sponge 66
Schwan, der swan 69
Schwanz, der tail 70
schwarz black 10
schweben float 29
Schwein, das pig 52
schwer hard 35
schwer heavy 36
Schwester, die sister 63
schwierig difficult 23
Schwimmbecken, das pool 54
schwimmen swim* 69
See, der lake 40
Seehund, der seal 61
Seestern, der starfish* 67
Seetang, der seaweed 61
Segelboot, das sailboat 59
segeln sail 59
sehen look 43
sehen see* 61
sehr very 76
Seife, die soap 65
Seifenblase, die bubble 13
Seifenlauge, die suds 68
Seil, das rope 58
sein be* 8
Seite, die page 50
Seite, die side 62
Sekretär, der secretary 61
Sekretärin, die secretary 61
Sellerie, der celery 16
Senf, der mustard 46
Serviette, die napkin 47
Sessel, der armchair 5
Shorts, die shorts 62
sicher safe 59
silbern silver 63
singen sing* 63
Sitz, der seat 61
sitzen sit* 63
Sitzgurt, der seatbelt 61
Ski, der ski 63
skilaufen ski 63
Smoking, der tuxedo 75
Socken, die socks 65
Sofa, das couch 20
Sofa, das sofa 65
Sohn, der son 65
Sommer, der summer 69
Sommersprossen, die freckles 31
Sonne, die sun 69
Sonnenaufgang, der sunrise 69
Sonnenuntergang, der sunset 69

Unkraut, das weed 78
unter below 9
unter beneath 9
unter bottom 11
unter under 75
Unterhaltung, die conversation 19
Unterkleid, das underwear 75
Unterricht, der lesson 42
Unterschrift, die signature 63
Unterseeboot, das submarine 68
Untertasse, die saucer 60

V

Vase, die vase 76
Vater, der father 28
Ventilator, der fan 27
Veranda, die porch 54
Verband, der bandage 7
verbeugen, sich bow 11
vergessen forget* 30
vergießen spill 66
verkaufen sell* 61
Verkehrsstau, der traffic jam 73
verlassen leave* 41
verletzen hurt* 37
Verwandte, der relative 57
Verwandte, die relative 57
viel much 46
viele many 44
vielen Dank thank you 71
Violine, die violin 76
Vogel, der bird 10
Vogelscheuche, die scarecrow 60
voll full 31
Volleyballspiel, das volleyball 76
von from 31
vor in front of 38
Vorhang, der curtain 21
vorsichtig careful 15

W

Waage, die scale 60
wachsen grow* 34
Waffel, die cone 19
Wagen, der wagon 76
Wald, der forest 30
Walfisch, der whale 78
Walroß, das walrus 77
Wand, die wall 77
wann when 78
warm warm 77
warten wait 76

Wartezimmer, das waiting room 76
was what 78
Wäsche, die laundry 41
waschen wash 77
Waschmaschine, die washing machine 77
Wasser, das water 77
Wasserfall, der waterfall 77
Wasserhahn, der faucet 28
Wassermelone, die watermelon 77
waten wade 76
Wecker, der alarm clock 4
Weg, der way 77
weg away 6
weich soft 65
Weide, die pasture 51
Weihnachtsmann, der Santa Claus 60
weinen cry 21
weiß white 78
weit far 27
Weizen, der wheat 78
Welle, die wave 77
Welt, die world 79
weniger less* 42
werden become* 9
werfen throw* 71
Werkstatt, die workshop 79
Werkzeugkasten, der toolbox 72
Wespe, die wasp 77
Wetter, das weather 78
Wettlauf, der race 56
wie how 37
wie like 42
willkommen welcome 78
Wind, der wind 79
winken wave 77
Winter, der winter 79
Wippe, die seesaw 61
wischen wipe 79
Wissenschaftler, der scientist 60
Wissenschaftlerin, die scientist 60
wo where 78
Woche, die week 78
wohnen live 43
Wohnzimmer, das living room 43
Wolf, der wolf* 79
Wolke, die cloud 18
Wolkenkratzer, der skyscraper 64
wollen want 77
Wort, das word 79
Wörterbuch, das dictionary 23
Würfel, der cube 21
Würfel, die dice* 23
Wurm, der worm 79

Wurst, die sausage 60
Wüste, die desert 22

X

Xylophon, das xylophone 80

Z

Zahn, der tooth* 72
Zahnarzt, der dentist 22
Zahnbürste, die toothbrush 72
Zähne, die teeth* 70
Zahnpaste, die toothpaste 73
Zauberer, der magician 44
Zaun, der fence 28
Zebra, das zebra 80
Zehe, die toe 72
zeichnen draw* 24
zeigen point 54
zeigen show* 62
zeigen, sich show* 62
Zeit, die time 72
Zeitschrift, die magazine 44
Zeitung, die newspaper 48
Zelt, das tent 71
zerbrechen break* 12
zerdrücken crush 21
Zicklein, das kid 40
Ziege, die goat 33
ziehen pull 55
Ziel, das target 70
Zimbel, die cymbal 21
Zimmer, das room 58
Zimmermann, der carpenter 15
Zirkus, der circus 17
Zirkuszelt, das big top 10
Zitrone, die lemon 42
Zoo, der zoo 80
Zopf, der braid 12
zu at 6
zu for 30
zu to 72
Zucker, der sugar 69
Zuckerwatte, die cotton candy 19
zuerst first 29
zufügen add 4
Zug, der train 73
Zügel, die reins 57
Zunge, die tongue 72
zusammen together 72
zusammen passen match 44
zuschauen watch 77
Zwiebel, die onion 49
zwischen between 9
Zylinder, der top hat 73